Who Killed Miracle?

Other Books by Scott Renyard

Illustrated Screenplays

The Pristine Coast (forthcoming fall 2022)

The Unofficial Trial of Alexandra Morton
(forthcoming fall 2022)

Trial of an Iconic Species (forthcoming winter 2023)

Children's Books

The Flag That Flew Up (2021)

WHO KILLED
MIRACLE?

an illustrated screenplay

SCOTT RENYARD

juggernaut CLASSICS

Published by Juggernaut Classics Inc.
Contact: scott@juggernautpictures.ca

ISBN: 978-1-7779157-4-2 (softcover)
ISBN: 978-1-7779157-5-9 (eBook)

Cover photograph by Brent Cooke
Photograph on page 2 by Rochelle Termehr
Edited by Lesley Cameron
Cover design by Michael George and Jan Westendorp
Book design by Jan Westendorp/katodesignandphoto.com

Juggernaut Classics Inc.

I dedicate this book to Miracle for her brave and informative life which has provided so much insight into the Southern Resident killer whale population. May her life not be in vain and that humans do what is needed to save Southern Resident killer whales from extinction.

Contents

Introduction

I N 1975, A FRIEND OF MINE, Richard Santos, helped me secure a part-time job at The Village Green Inn in Vernon, British Columbia. I worked in the kitchen there for five years, part-time during the school year and full-time during the summers and Christmas holidays. I gradually moved up the ranks and learned how to make everything that appeared on the menus of both the hotel coffee shop and the Hy's Steak House: salads, desserts, main courses, and even hollandaise sauce. I left my job and kitchen friends behind when I moved to Vancouver in 1979 to pursue a bachelor's degree in science at the University of British Columbia.

By 1984 I was working on a master's degree through the UBC School of Community and Regional Planning. My expectation was that I would one day become a regional planner somewhere in BC. I loaded up my schedule with a broad range of classes, but I was most drawn to fishery and forestry issues. My thesis, "A Planned Strategy for Developing Burrard Inlet's Shore-based Sport Fisheries," was an investigation of the fishing activity I first noticed at Jericho Pier, near the UBC Endowment Lands. I later co-published "Sport Angler Preferences for Alternative Regulatory Methods" with Ray Hilborn, my UBC directed studies professor, in the prestigious *Canadian Journal of Fisheries and Aquatic Sciences*. I felt I was on the way to a career in science research and study.

Then, one day, an old friend and colleague from my Village Green Inn days, Rick Cavazzi, called up and asked if I would like to make salads and desserts for a film crew. He had already hired Richard Santos. Even though I was just scraping by on a tight budget as a student, I wasn't really looking for just any job. I had just finished my final exams and was searching for a summer job that would support my career goals. But when he told me they were paying $900.00 a week, I was in. At that time, $900.00 a week was a lot of money for anyone, never mind a student who had less than a week's wages in the bank. So, suddenly the three of us were reunited as cooks. On my first day on the job, I was told, "Oh, and by the way, we want you to drive a truck." "Sure, no problem," I said blithely. I thought I would be driving one of those food trucks you see on the streets.

The next day, I showed up at a field in Surrey, BC, and met with the owners of the catering company. "Which truck am I supposed to drive?" I asked them. They told me to go to the old Bridge manufacturing property on Boundary Road the next day and they would introduce me to the truck. It turned out it was no food truck. It was a 30-foot tractor-trailer unit. I had never even been a passenger in a truck that size, never mind a driver. But I really wanted the $900.00 a week, so I asked, "When do we move?" It wouldn't be for two weeks. "Sure, no problem. I can drive it," I told them. As soon as the owners were gone, I had one of the Teamster drivers on the show teach me how to disconnect the tractor, and I practised driving the old beast on the land now occupied by The Bridge Studios in Burnaby.

In the end, we were fired as caterers, not because of my truck driving or the quality of the meals, but because our food costs were too high. Imagine that. Well, the catering company owed me some money, and the shop steward for the Teamsters recommended I talk to the union. Little did I realize the Teamsters were trying to unionize the caterers, and my dispute went a long way to making that happen. A compromise was struck, and I ended up as Bonnie Bedila's driver. At the time, I just wanted the money owed to me. But that decision to grant me union membership completely changed my career path and launched me into the film industry.

By the mid-1990s I had worked on many large productions in various capacities, but primarily in transportation. While working on the

Neon Rider series, I became Winston Rekert's assistant and was tasked with reading scripts, producing reader's reports, coordinating publicity, and assisting with post-production. After reading several hundred scripts, I began writing some of my own. I remember a gag I pulled on a series called *The New Adventures of Beans Baxter*. I wrote a spec script and gave it to some of the series department heads, telling them it might be a script coming up, just to see if my writing was any good. A couple of days later, I went back and asked what they thought of the script. Some of them had started prepping it as though it was the next script. Of course, it wasn't bought or made into an episode. All the episodes were already under contract with writers, so it didn't have a chance. But the fact that my writing was considered by the show's production staff as comparable to the production scripts spurred me on. Shortly after that, I began writing original stories. It wasn't long before I had an agent and began another new career, this time as a scriptwriter.

The process of waiting for a script to make it to the screen was torturously long. I went to seminars and made a trek to the Banff Television Festival several years in a row to better understand Canada's domestic film industry. My goal was to find a way to get my scripts made into a film. But the first trip threw me a curve ball. I had spent most of my early career on expensive, large budget shows. Now I was suddenly exposed to the world of documentary film making.

The format was intriguing in two ways. First, the stories were, of course, based on fact. And that appealed to my inner scientist. Second, documentaries were relatively cheap compared to other formats. After my first couple of visits to the Banff festival, the word got around on the *Neon Rider* series that I was working on documentaries. I then had a bit of a breakthrough when Winston asked me to do a documentary about the *Neon Rider* series as the last episode. The contract was signed, and I began outlining the story for the documentary episode. It was very exciting—until the network told the producers that they couldn't do documentary in a drama slot. It was going to mess up their Canadian content requirements. The documentary was a no go. So they asked me to pivot the story into a drama clip show. I was thrilled to do so, since writing a drama was my original goal. And it was a fun and rewarding experience. The trouble was, the show was over and one episode was not enough for me to break into the world of drama series writers. Over the next year or two, I sold a couple of original scripts, but it didn't look like they were going to be put into production. So I had to look for ways to move forward with my new career.

After several years of study and attendance at many seminars, I began to "find my voice," as many people in the business say. I came to realize that even though I wanted to participate in the world of fictional storytelling, I also wanted to tell stories that would use both my science education and my film experience. Many film makers start their careers by making documentaries and use that as leverage to move into fiction. I found myself doing the opposite.

One piece of advice I heard over and over was "Write what you know." I would extend this to include "Make films about stories that you know or have researched well and subjects that you adore." You want to have a strong connection to the subject, because it's a lot of work to make a film and the project often takes years to complete. And once the film is done, it will be with you for the rest of your life. It's a lot like being a musician who has a hit and then has to sing their hit song for years and years afterward.

In 1999, at our family Thanksgiving dinner, I told my mom that I was looking for a good environmental/nature story. To my surprise, she said there was a story under her bed that might work. She disappeared for a few minutes, then presented me with a dusty old shoebox. In it were three blue canisters of 8 mm footage marked "Miracle." Of course, I asked, "What's this?" "Well," she said, "this is the footage Peter took of the baby killer whale that was rescued by Sealand."

It turned out my stepdad, Peter Termehr, had been given permission in 1977 by Bob Wright, owner of Sealand of the Pacific, to film the rehabilitation of a baby killer whale that was rescued from Menzies Bay near Campbell River on Vancouver Island, BC. The footage had been collecting dust under Mom's bed since 1982.

The baby whale had been shot and was slowly dying in Menzies Bay. Bob pulled together a team of veterinarians and staff to rescue it. The rescue was a logistical nightmare. The whale's location was a four-hour drive north of Victoria, BC, where Sealand was located. The team travelled through the night with a flat-deck truck and equipment to capture the whale.

Once Miracle, as the whale became known, was captured and loaded onto the truck, the Sealand team realized they needed to put her somewhere near Sealand. They didn't want to put her in with the other animals in case she had any infectious diseases. So they approached the old Oak Bay Beach Hotel, just down the street, as it had an abandoned outdoor saltwater pool. They got permission to quickly fix up the pool and then plunked the sick and injured whale into it so they could offer her round-the-clock intensive care. But the first few hours did not go well. Miracle sank to the bottom, and her handlers needed to hold her up to the surface so she could breathe.

The 8 mm reels weren't an obsolete format, but it wasn't easy finding someone who could transfer the footage to digital files, which had become the standard format by then. After a few weeks of networking, I found a young man who transferred 8 mm footage in his basement suite. His jerry-rigged set-up did a marvellous job, and within a month I finally got my first look at the footage. It was amazing, and I knew immediately it was the backbone of a film.

As it turned out, the story began several weeks before Sealand was called in to help rescue the baby whale. Miracle was first seen swimming alone near Nanaimo, BC, in a frantic and erratic manner. It's rare to see a juvenile killer whale alone. A few weeks later, she was spotted swimming slowly 160 kilometres north in Menzies Bay, near Campbell River. Bill Davis, a sport fisherman who lived in Campbell River, had been told to watch out for a whale in the bay. His curiosity got the better of him, and he went looking for the whale. Bill found her and realized that not only was she a very young whale but she also looked like she was in trouble. After watching her for a few minutes, he decided to try to feed her some herring he was using for bait. To his surprise, she came up and ate the first one he tossed in the water. After that, Bill held onto the fish until the whale took it right out of his hand. Soon the little whale trusted him so much he was able to pet her. This remarkable bond, formed between a fisherman and a wild killer whale, was the first of its kind. But Bill realized the whale needed help, so he called the Vancouver Aquarium and talked to its director, Murray Newman, who, in turn, called Dr. Michael Bigg, head of killer whale research at the Pacific Biological Station in Naniamo. Bigg called on Sealand to help, as he knew it had the resources they would need.

Miracle's rehabilitation lasted for more than six months in the Oak Bay Beach Hotel pool. But as Miracle recovered from her injuries and started to grow, Sealand realized she needed to be moved from the hotel pool to a new pool at Sealand. Her handlers remembered how close she had come to dying from the ride on the truck to Oak Bay and wanted to make sure the move went as quickly as possible. So they decided to move her by helicopter. What an event it was. Thousands of people came out to watch.

The move to the new pool was a success. But Miracle subsequently became the subject of a political fight. Animal rights groups wanted her to go free. They even held a press conference at the side of the Oak Bay Beach Hotel pool. The controversy pushed Sealand to add security features like double nets to their pools. The fight went on for four years until, tragically, Miracle was found dead at the bottom of her pool.

The newspaper headlines stated that Miracle had likely drowned during a botched plot to free her. This triggered even more debate about captive whales and whether or not Miracle should have been set free years earlier. It was bitterly ironic that she would die by the hands of people who were trying to help her.

I wondered if I could find out who was responsible. So, this story, for me, began to take the form of a real-life murder mystery about an amazing baby killer whale named Miracle. I started by interviewing the principle characters involved in her rescue and rehabilitation. Several interviewees seemed unsettled when I asked, "How did she die?" I began to suspect that there was more to the story than the media had reported and sought out more people involved in Miracle's life. That was how I discovered her death was not due to sabotage gone wrong. The cause of her death was more complicated than that, and it involved her natural instincts, the threat of someone trying to free her, the design of the pool, and Sealand staff's errors and fears. As Larry McInerney says, "It's not the one thing that gets you, it's the combination of things that get you." Everyone loved Miracle, and no one wanted her to die at such a young age. But it still happened.

The film went on to win a few awards and was recognized for its insights into killer whale behaviour. I am proud that I was able to unravel much of the mystery surrounding Miracle's life and, in particular, her death. During filming, many of the interview subjects became quite emotional about the loss of Miracle. She affected so many in a profound way and taught us so much about her species.

Miracle also had a tremendous effect on my life. Her story became the first film I completed where I was creatively in charge from the concept to the completion of the project. I credit this film as the project that not only helped me find my voice, but also revealed to me how I could use both my science background and my passion for film making to create a satisfying career for myself. And all because I said yes to a catering job that helped me finance the last few months of my education.

Cast of Characters

(In Order of Appearance)

LARRY MCINERNEY:
Former Head Diver, Sealand of the Pacific

BILL DAVIS:
Sport Fisherman, Campbell River resident

ANGUS MATTHEWS:
Former General Manager, Sealand of the Pacific

PAUL WATSON:
Founder, Sea Shepherd Conservation Society

PATRICK MOORE:
Former President, Greenpeace Canada

ALEXANDRA MORTON:
Former Volunteer, Sealand of the Pacific

DR. ALLAN HOEY:
Former Head Veterinarian, Sealand of the Pacific

NARRATOR:
August Schellenberg

BOB WRIGHT:
Former Owner, Sealand of the Pacific

(continued on following page)

DR. LANCE BARRETT-LENNARD:
Orca Researcher and Geneticist, University
of British Columbia

GRAEME ELLIS:
Head of Orca Research, Department of
Fisheries and Oceans, Pacific

UN-NAMED WOMAN:
Victoria Resident

BRUCE BOTT:
Whale Activist

DR. PETER ROSS:
Former Marine Mammal Toxicologist,
Institute of Ocean Sciences

Who Killed Miracle?
—an illustrated screenplay

by
Scott Renyard

FADE IN:

EXT. REMOTE PACIFIC COAST — DAY

Killer whales surface and take a breath.

TITLE: Juggernaut Pictures presents . . .

A series of killer whale shots in the wild.

TITLE: A Who Killed Miracle Production

More whales surface. Then one leaps into the air. Another spy hops.

TITLE: Written and Directed by Scott Renyard

A killer whale flips its tail.

TITLE: Edited by Maja Zdanowski

A pod surfaces and dives.

TITLE: Original Score by Heather Kemski

UNDERWATER — A killer whale spins slowly.

TITLE: Narrated by August Schellenberg

A spectacular dusk shot of killer whales surfacing, taking a breath and diving underwater.

FADE TO:

LOOKING UP — The sun is visible through eerie, murky green water.

TITLE: A wavy "Who Killed Miracle?" appears.

UNDERWATER — Murky green water. Seaweed. Eerie.

SUPERSCRIPT: January 12, 1982.

Classical music creates a mood that something terrible has happened.

AND WE GO TO:

AN UNDERWATER NET — Algae is growing on it.

> LARRY MCINERNEY (V.O.)
> I think it was about 3:30 or 4 o'clock, just before I went home, I went down there, and I saw her and . . .

INT. LARRY MCINERNEY'S HOUSE — DAY

> LARRY MCINERNEY
> . . . she dove straight down. She was right in the middle of the pool . . .

ON A NET — It runs off into the distance underwater.

Miracle dives straight down in her pool. (Photo credit: Brent Cooke)

> LARRY MCINERNEY (V.O.)
> . . . it was sort of an
> abnormal behaviour for her,
> but I thought, "Oh yeah,
> she's got that ball again,
> that's what she's playing
> with." . . .

Divers swimming underwater with bubbles
floating around. Eerie.

> LARRY MCINERNEY (V.O.)
> . . . I got home and I got
> a phone call and it said
> that . . .

BACK TO LARRY

> LARRY MCINERNEY
> . . . uh, the whale, uh,
> wasn't there, so . . .

CLOSE ON THE NET — The sun slices through the
net and the green water.

We realize the diver is Larry.

> LARRY MCINERNEY (V.O.)
> . . . so I got back there
> and I got my diving gear on,
> jumped in the pool and swam
> down to the bottom. What I
> found was a huge hole . . .

ANGLE — A hole in a chain-link fence.

          LARRY MCINERNEY (V.O.)
     . . . and she was just sort
     of wrapped in this cargo
     net . . .

BACK TO LARRY

Larry's chin quivers. He's close to tears.

          LARRY MCINERNEY (V.O.)
     . . . She drowned, and uh,
     that was basically it for
     that.

The music builds. Bubbles rise from the
depths through the frame.

                         FADE TO:

INT. BILL DAVIS'S LIVING ROOM — DAY

Bill Davis, sport fisherman, tells us what he
believes happened to Miracle.

          BILL DAVIS
     Well, yes, we know how she
     died. Ah . . .

INT. OCEAN — DUSK

Two divers swimming side by side like shadows
move down to an underwater chain-link fence.
Their flashlight shines through the water.

                    BILL DAVIS (V.O.)
              . . . some divers got in the
              water in the marina . . .

CLOSE ON — The diver's hands are visible as
he cuts a hole in the net.

                    BILL DAVIS (V.O.)
              . . . dove under and cut a
              hole through the outside
              netting of her pen and cut a
              hole through the inside . . .

WIDER

The two divers cut away at the chain-link
fence.

                    BILL DAVIS (V.O.)
              . . . And of course, the whale
              being as tame as what she
              is . . .

BACK TO BILL

                    BILL DAVIS
              . . . Miracle is her name,
              what she was, she thought it
              was probably someone to play
              with and she went down . . .

BACK TO THE DIVERS

They swim away from the hole.

>   BILL DAVIS (V.O.)
>   . . . and got through the nets
>   and got caught in between the
>   two nets and couldn't come up
>   for air and drowned.

Another piece of cut net floats by.

>   ANGUS MATTHEWS (V.O.)
>   Essentially what happened is
>   something I think we're going
>   to have real trouble figuring
>   out.

EXT. SHORE — DAY

Angus Matthews, former Sealand of the Pacific
aquarium general manager, is sitting on a
rock.

>   ANGUS MATTHEWS
>   There is so many possibilities.
>   There were those who wanted
>   the whale free . . . um . . .

NEWS HEADLINES — "Whale campaign worries
Sealand," "Tug-of-War looms," "Miracle's pool
net cut — but how is a mystery" move slowly
across the screen.

                    ANGUS MATTHEWS (V.O.)
          . . . There were those that
          were determined to make that
          happen. Whether they were
          successful, and whether they
          were responsible, we never had
          any way of finding out . . .

BACK TO ANGUS

                    ANGUS MATTHEWS
          . . . There were rumours,
          there were theories, there
          were suspicions . . .

BACK TO THE DIVERS

The divers are cutting the fence and peering
into the hole with a flashlight to see what
they are doing.

CLOSE ON — The divers use their bolt cutters,
snapping through the links.

                    PAUL WATSON (V.O.)
          Or whether it's people acting
          irresponsibly, even though
          their motivations was quite,
          maybe, ideal which is to try
          and free the animal . . .

INT. ROOM — DAY

Paul Watson, Sea Shepherd founder, tells us
what he knows.

                    PAUL WATSON
          . . . even though they didn't
          take into account . . . that
          . . . the consequences of . . .

EXT. SEINER (JANUARY 1982) — DAY

It drifts away on the ocean.

ON THE DECK

Miracle is lying on her side. People are
milling around. A young Angus is talking with
someone next to Miracle's body.

                    PAUL WATSON (V.O.)
          . . . that action. The fact is,
          they committed a crime . . .
          a whale died, they were
          responsible . . .

A diver swims through the green murky water
and lurks near a sagging net.

                    PAUL WATSON (V.O.)
          . . . for the death of the
          whale. And from our point of
          view . . .

BACK TO THE DIVERS PULLING THE HOLE OPEN

                    PAUL WATSON (V.O.)
          . . . as an organization that
          is policing this . . .

BACK TO PAUL

>PAUL WATSON
>. . . that's why we were
>involved in it, that's why
>we made that information
>available to the public.

A cut net drifts by.

FADE TO:

EXT. STREET (CBC ARCHIVE) — DAY

>PATRICK MOORE
>I say to that person, whoever
>they are, if they were indeed
>involved in foul play to
>release Miracle . . .

NEWS HEADLINES — "Probe finds Miracle drowned
but death can't be explained," "Mystery
caller claims role in death," "Phone caller
claims to cut Miracle's net," and "Was
Miracle's net cut?"

>PATRICK MOORE (V.O.)
>. . . that they should
>come forward and identify
>themselves if they are so
>guilt-stricken and face the
>music because I don't like the
>fact that Greenpeace is being
>implicated in this due to some
>anonymous phone caller.

INT. VANCOUVER AQUARIUM LAB — DAY

Alexandra Morton, killer whale researcher, reveals what she suspects happened to Miracle.

> ALEXANDRA MORTON
> I was told that she'd gotten trapped between the inner net and the outer net . . .

MONTAGE — Nets underwater, drifting mesh.

> ALEXANDRA MORTON (V.O.)
> . . . because she had two nets. One net for her pen and there was a big net that, I guess, went around the whole park. And ah . . .

BACK TO ALEXANDRA

> ALEXANDRA MORTON
> . . . Sealand was saying someone had cut the net.

ANGLE — More net mesh weaves through the water.

> ALLAN HOEY (V.O.)
> I just got the shocking phone call that saying, ah, that she had drowned . . .

EXT. ANOTHER SHORE — DAY

Allan Hoey, Sealand veterinarian, sits in a chair, next to the old Oak Bay Beach Hotel pool and the ocean.

                    ALLAN HOEY
          . . . It was just
          heartbreaking to have gone
          through all the work that we
          did . . .

BACK TO THE SEINER

A young Angus runs his fingers through his hair.

                    ALLAN HOEY (V.O.)
          . . . the rescue, saving this
          animal and then, bingo, ah,
          suddenly gone.

A necropsy of Miracle is underway. Her body has been opened up as part of the investigation into cause of death.

EXT. MIRACLE'S SEALAND POOL — DAY

Miracle moves slowly to the surface and breathes out. Then she leaps up and creates a big splash as she re-enters the water. She turns in the water and we freeze on Miracle as the footage runs off the end of the reel.

                                        FADE TO:

INT. MENZIES BAY — DAY

A murky green world of floating marine snow and seaweed.

SUPERSCRIPT: Four-and-a-half years earlier, August 6, 1977.

A small rock fish swims through the algae.

EXT. MENZIES BAY — DAY

Bill starts up his boat.

>   BILL DAVIS (V.O.)
>   Just as we were launching the
>   boat, this young girl, oh, I
>   guess she was 10 or 11 years
>   old . . .

Bill turns the boat near a log boom.

>   BILL DAVIS (V.O.)
>   . . . said, "Don't go down
>   into the bay." She said,
>   "There is a killer whale down
>   there." . . .

BILL POV

The nose of his little boat cruising out into Menzies Bay.

>   BILL DAVIS (V.O.)
>   . . . As it turned out, fishing
>   wasn't so hot that night . . .

INT. BILL DAVIS'S LIVING ROOM — DAY

>   BILL DAVIS
>   . . . so we decided to take a
>   run down and have a look at
>   this whale, and that's when I
>   found her there . . .

**LOWER THIRD: Bill Davis, sport fisherman and
Campbell River resident.**

EXT. MENZIES BAY (AUGUST 1977) — AFTERNOON

People in a boat look at Miracle swimming
around them. Miracle surfaces just a few feet
from a boat.

>   BILL DAVIS (V.O.)
>   . . . It made me wonder at
>   that time, why I could see
>   it was a young whale, why
>   she'd just be swimming by
>   herself . . .

The small whale comes to the surface, barely
swimming. It's clear she's very young and not
healthy.

VERY CLOSE

A melon and blowhole emerge through the surface. The whale is covered in a brown algae.

>   BILL DAVIS (V.O.)
>   . . . By this time I could see
>   that she was all covered with
>   brown. I didn't know what it
>   was.

Another boat filled with a family floats near the little whale. Miracle comes to the surface and grabs a dead herring floating in the water.

>   NARRATOR (V.O.)
>   The average person would've
>   taken note of the sick whale
>   and perhaps reported it to the
>   authorities . . .

EXT. MENZIES BAY — LATER

Bill races across the bay in his boat.

>   NARRATOR (V.O.)
>   . . . But Bill's instinct was
>   to stay and try to help the
>   whale.

Bill drifts around in his boat.

                    BILL DAVIS (V.O.)
          Well, I just drifted, just
          drifted around and then she
          got closer to the boat. And
          I thought, well, I had some
          herring I was going to use
          for my fishing. I threw it
          out . . .

MIRACLE POV

A herring floats down from the surface toward
her with Bill and his boat above. Bill throws
out a herring and it slowly sinks.

                    BILL DAVIS (V.O.)
          . . . She didn't come right
          away, but a few minutes later
          I saw her. She came up behind
          the boat and picked this
          up . . .

FROM ABOVE

Miracle approaches Bill's boat and eats a
herring. Then she surfaces near the other
boat with the family in it.

                    BILL DAVIS (V.O.)
          . . . And by the time I'd used
          all my bait up, she'd . . .
          she was getting quite close,
          about 20 to 30 feet from the
          boat . . .

Miracle surfaces close to the boat. And then swims slowly by Bill's boat.

> BILL DAVIS
> . . . and every time I threw one out, she'd turn around, come back and pick another one up, wait for another one, so it was getting quite exciting at that time . . .

PHOTO — Miracle with Bill's shadow reflecting in the water.

> BILL DAVIS (V.O.)
> . . . And by this time I could see she was covered with plankton or whatever was on her body and . . .

PHOTO — Miracle's back and scratches on her back.

> BILL DAVIS (V.O.)
> . . . I could see she had a wound of some sort when she came up.

ON BILL

He throttles up his boat and exits.

                    NARRATOR (V.O.)
          Realizing the young whale was
          sick, Davis decided to return
          with more herring and hoped
          that all she needed was food.

MIRACLE POV

She sees Bill return in his boat.

                    BILL DAVIS (V.O.)
          About seven o'clock at night,
          and I went down there, and
          right away she didn't seem to
          be worried about the boat at
          all . . .

She swims up from the depths toward a herring
dangling from Bill's fingers.

                    BILL DAVIS (V.O.)
          . . . I think that was the
          first night she started to come
          right up and I could get her
          to take it out of my hand. I'd
          hold herring over the, over
          the water . . .

BILL POV

Miracle comes up and takes the herring out of
Bill's fingers.

> BILL DAVIS (V.O.)
> . . . I'd hold my end and
> she'd get a hold of the
> other . . .

INT. BILL DAVIS'S LIVING ROOM — DAY

Bill smiles as he remembers the encounter.

> BILL DAVIS
> . . . I guess she was about
> as afraid of me as I was of
> her . . .

EXT. MENZIES BAY — DAY

Miracle takes a breath near Bill's boat.

> BILL DAVIS (V.O.)
> . . . Then, I believe, it was
> the second night that . . .

INT. OCEAN — NEXT DAY

LOOKING UP AT BILL'S BOAT.

> BILL DAVIS (V.O.)
> . . . I could hold the herring
> up and put the other hand out
> over the water and . . .

PHOTO — Miracle swims near Bill's boat.

> BILL DAVIS (V.O.)
> . . . I wouldn't give her a
> herring until she, I got my
> hand on her, after that . . .

PHOTO — Bill reaches off the back of his boat
and pets Miracle.

> BILL DAVIS (V.O.)
> . . . I rubbed her a little
> bit, after that, and it was
> no problem. She let me touch
> her . . .

PHOTO — Bill reaches out and gives Miracle a
herring.

> NARRATOR (V.O.)
> Bill's friendship with the
> baby killer whale made
> history. This was the first
> time on record that a killer
> whale had allowed a human to
> feed it . . .

PHOTO — Bill reaches over and pets Miracle.

> NARRATOR (V.O.)
> . . . by hand in the wild. And
> this came at a time when most
> people were still afraid of
> killer whales.

INT. BILL DAVIS'S LIVING ROOM — LATER

                    BILL DAVIS
        The third day, when I came
        down there, I could see her
        in the distance, quite aways,
        well, as soon as she heard
        the motor coming down, she
        actually came to meet me . . .
                                    FADE TO:

PHOTO — Bill with friends in his boat.

INT. OCEAN — EVENING

MIRACLE POV — She swims through murky water
around Bill's boat.

                    BILL DAVIS (V.O.)
        . . . After I fed her, I just
        pulled away quite slowly
        and she kept following the
        boat. So, I had a few herring
        left . . .

ON THE BOAT PROPELLER — Bubbles blast as Bill
takes off.

                    BILL DAVIS (V.O.)
        . . . So I just threw them in
        the water quite quickly and
        took off with the motor so I
        could get away from her . . .

INT. BILL DAVIS'S LIVING ROOM — DAY

Bill Davis, Campbell River sport fisherman, feeds Miracle, a baby killer whale, in Menzies Bay, August 1977. (Photo credit: Campbell River Museum)

Miracle swims alone in Menzies Bay near Campbell River, BC. (Photo credit: Bill Davis)

                    BILL DAVIS
        . . . And that's what I had to
        do after that.

EXT. MENZIES BAY (AUGUST 1977) — DAY

Miracle swims slowly out in the bay by
herself. She turns awkwardly in the water.

PHOTO — Miracle peeks out of the water.

                    NARRATOR (V.O.)
          Word travelled fast in the
          small town of Campbell River
          that Davis was feeding a
          killer whale by hand in
          Menzies Bay.

Miracle is barely swimming.

WIDER

A boat full of curious onlookers gets close
to Miracle.

                    BILL DAVIS (V.O.)
          After a couple of days of
          this down there, I realized
          I wasn't going to be able to
          continue to feed her. So it
          wasn't very long before the
          news got out.

PHOTO — Miracle takes a breath.

                    NARRATOR (V.O.)
          Davis realized that the little
          whale was quickly becoming
          accustomed to boats . . .

ANGLE — Miracle swims very close to the
boats.

                    NARRATOR (V.O.)
          . . . And with the increasing
          numbers of onlookers, he was
          afraid someone would run over
          her . . .

PHOTO — Miracle swims in Menzies Bay, alone
for now.

INT. OFFICE (1977) — DAY

Dr. Murray Newman, executive director of the
Vancouver Aquarium, is being interviewed.

                    BILL DAVIS (V.O.)
          I didn't know anybody to
          contact. I had met Dr. Newman
          in the Vancouver Aquarium,
          he'd been up here at meetings
          and I had met him. I thought,
          well . . .

BACK TO BILL

> BILL DAVIS (V.O.)
> . . . he would be a person to
> phone.

MAP — Vancouver Island and southwest British
Columbia.

The names of the cities Vancouver, Campbell
River, Nanaimo and Victoria appear.

> NARRATOR (V.O.)
> Davis's phone call to the
> Vancouver Aquarium and Murray
> Newman . . .

An arrow goes from Campbell River to
Vancouver.

> NARRATOR (V.O.)
> . . . was the first of three
> calls. Newman then called Dr.
> Michael Bigg . . .

A second arrow goes from Vancouver to
Nanaimo.

> NARRATOR (V.O.)
> . . . head of killer whale
> research at the Pacific
> Biological Station in
> Nanaimo . . .

A third arrow goes to Nanaimo.

                    NARRATOR (V.O.)
          . . . Bigg, in turn, called
          the one man on Vancouver
          Island with the resources and
          expertise to rescue a killer
          whale.

EXT. OAK BAY MARINA — DAY

Establish.

ON A WHARF

Bob Wright is sitting on a dock with
sunglasses on.

**LOWER THIRD: Robert (Bob) Wright, former
owner, Sealand of the Pacific.**

                    BOB WRIGHT
          And they asked if I would go
          up and take a look at it and
          see what I could do . . .

PHOTO — Head shot of Bill Davis.

PHOTO — Bill feeds Miracle by hand.

                    BOB WRIGHT (V.O.)
          . . . And the story was that
          there was a chap up there
          feeding it by hand. We quite
          frankly believed that somebody
          had . . .

BACK TO BOB

>   BOB WRIGHT
> . . . made a misinterpretation
> on what the animal really
> was . . .

PHOTO — Miracle in Menzies Bay.

>   BOB WRIGHT (V.O.)
> . . . I questioned him fully
> at the time whether it had
> ears or had spots like a seal.
> He said, "No. I know a killer
> whale. It's a killer whale."

                                    FADE TO:

PHOTO — Miracle swims at the surface in
Menzies Bay.

EXT. SHORE — DAY

Angus Matthews is sitting on a rock next to
the ocean.

**LOWER THIRD: Angus Matthews, former General
Manager, Sealand of the Pacific, Victoria,
British Columbia.**

>   ANGUS MATTHEWS
> None of us believed it was
> possible. It never happened
> anywhere in the world
> before . . .

PHOTO — Bill with a passenger in his boat.
He's feeding Miracle.

>   ANGUS MATTHEWS (V.O.)
>   . . . that a killer whale had
>   relied on an individual to
>   feed him and hand-feed him.

FROM UNDERWATER — Bill looks down into the
water as a herring drifts away from him.

>   FADE TO:

EXT. SKY — AFTERNOON

A seaplane motors out of Victoria Harbour to
ready for takeoff.

>   NARRATOR (V.O.)
>   In spite of their skepticism,
>   Wright hired a float plane and
>   flew to Nanaimo, picking up
>   Dr. Bigg on the way to Menzies
>   Bay . . .

EXT. HILL — AFTERNOON

A wide view of Menzies Bay.

>   NARRATOR (V.O.)
>   . . . Once they arrived and
>   found Bill Davis . . .

BOAT POV — A boat races across the bay.

> NARRATOR (V.O.)
> . . . They went out on the
> water to see the creature Bill
> had been feeding by hand.

INT. BILL DAVIS'S LIVING ROOM — AFTERNOON

> BILL DAVIS
> I got in there and I stopped
> the motor. . . and I thought,
> she's got to come . . .
> ur . . .

MIRACLE POV — Miracle peeks out of the water
at Bill's boat.

> BILL DAVIS (V.O.)
> . . . somewhere, and there was
> no sign, well, maybe, I should
> start the motor up.

EXT. OCEAN — MOMENTS LATER

No sign of Miracle. Bill cruises by in his
boat.

> NARRATOR (V.O.)
> The Sealand group thought
> Davis was crazy to think that
> a killer whale would respond
> to the sound of a boat . . .

UNDERWATER — Bill engages the propeller.

> NARRATOR (V.O.)
> . . . But with no whale in
> sight, he started up the
> engine.

ANOTHER ANGLE — Suddenly Miracle appears just
under the surface.

> ANGUS MATTHEWS (V.O.)
> It was just a ripple on the
> surface, and just a glimmer
> of a shape, and it just broke
> surface and disappeared
> again . . .

BACK TO ANGUS

> ANGUS MATTHEWS
> . . . It was impossible to
> tell what it was . . .

Miracle surfaces quickly and disappears
again.

> ANGUS MATTHEWS (V.O.)
> . . . And it wasn't until it
> surfaced a third or fourth
> time with just the water . . .

Miracle then turns and just comes to the
surface. She takes a small breath.

              ANGUS MATTHEWS (V.O.)
     . . . bulging up above it
     and just coming through and
     then a breath being taken.
     And the breath was so faint,
     it almost sounded more like
     a person breathing. It was
     Jay that looked down and Jay
     said, "It's a killer whale."
     And that was the first time we
     really came face to face with
     a creature that was actually
     going . . .

PHOTO — Dr. Jay Hyman leans over in Bill
Davis's boat and sees Miracle.

BACK TO ANGUS

              ANGUS MATTHEWS
     . . . to transform not just
     our lives but the lives of the
     whole community of Victoria
     and Campbell River over the
     next seven months.

PHOTO — Bill tips the boat to feed Miracle.

              BILL DAVIS (V.O.)
     During the course of feeding
     her, Bob said, "Well, I wonder
     if I could feed her." . . .

PHOTO — Miracle drifts by at the surface.

Bill Davis and Dr. Jay Hyman, a member of Sealand's rescue crew, look for Miracle. (Photo credit: Campbell River Museum)

>   BILL DAVIS (V.O.)
> . . . I said, "Well, we'll try
> it." So he took out a herring
> and held it out but she was
> reluctant to take it . . .

BACK TO MIRACLE — She is covered in algae.
She takes a breath.

>   BILL DAVIS (V.O.)
> . . . But then he came back to
> where I was, and I'd hold my
> hand out . . .

PHOTO — Miracle takes a herring from the
cigar-smoking Bob Wright.

>   BILL DAVIS (V.O.)
> . . . he'd put his hand out,
> and pretty soon she'd take it
> from me, then she'd take one
> from him . . .

INT. BILL DAVIS'S LIVING ROOM — DAY

>   BILL DAVIS
> . . . She adapted quite well
> to strangers as well.

PHOTO — Bill and Bob in a boat tied up to a
log in Menzies Bay.

Miracle comes right up to the boat and Bill Davis pets her while
Dr. Jay Hyman watches in amazement. (Photo credit: Campbell River Museum)

ANGUS MATTHEWS (V.O.)
Well, it was Jay's
instructions . . .

PHOTO — Dr. Jay Hyman looks at Miracle.

ANGUS MATTHEWS (V.O.)
. . . that if this animal was
to survive, immediate action
was required . . .

ANGLE — Miracle makes a slow surface near the
boats.

BILL DAVIS (V.O.)
I think at that time Dr. Hyman
said, "Well, Bob, it may
not be advisable to do that
because if something happened
to her and . . .

PHOTO — Miracle at the surface. She has
visible scars.

BILL DAVIS (V.O.)
. . . she did die on the way
to Victoria . . .

PHOTO — Miracle has a small spray of water
from her blowhole.

BILL DAVIS (V.O.)
. . . well, a lot of people
wouldn't be very happy about
that . . .

BACK TO PHOTO — Bob Wright holds out a
herring for Miracle.

> BILL DAVIS (V.O.)
> . . . But after Bob fed her
> herring a few times, and he
> was able to touch her, he
> thought . . .

BACK TO BILL

> BILL DAVIS
> . . . he'd just go ahead and
> do it anyway.

PHOTO — Miracle takes a breath near Bill's
boat.

> NARRATOR (V.O.)
> Three things had to happen
> before the rescue could
> proceed . . .

PHOTO — Dr. Michael Bigg.

> NARRATOR (V.O.)
> Dr. Bigg had to give federal
> government approval . . .

EXT. SEALAND OF THE PACIFIC (1977) — DAY

Bob Wright watches over his animals.

                    NARRATOR (V.O)
          . . . Bob Wright had to
          be willing to spend the
          money . . .

PHOTO — Bill Davis.

                    NARRATOR (V.O.)
          . . . and Bill Davis had to
          agree that "his" whale needed
          help . . .

BACK TO MIRACLE — She takes a breath in
Menzies Bay.

                    NARRATOR (V.O.)
          . . . When all three agreed,
          Sealand quickly assembled a
          rescue team.
                                        FADE TO:

EXT. PARKING LOT (SLOW MOTION) — DAY

A skill saw, lumber and nets are tossed onto
the back of a flat-deck truck.

                    ANGUS MATTHEWS
          A crazy friend of mine is a
          logger, and a man about town,
          house mover, you name it, he's
          done it, Ritchie Parken . . .

ON THE TIRE — Someone opens the passenger
door and gets in.

                    ANGUS MATTHEWS (V.O.)
          . . . Since he was on Bob
          Wright's expense account, he
          bought all new tools, bought
          a generator, put it all on
          the back of the truck, and
          he actually wore a logger's
          safety belt and clipped it to
          the truck . . .

ON THE MIRROR — The truck moves down the
road.

                    ANGUS MATTHEWS (V.O.)
          . . . and as the truck was
          driving to Campbell River, he
          was on the back of it with the
          skill saw and tools, actually
          building the crate . . .

PHOTO — The crew puts together the last prep
on the back of the truck in the dark.

                    ANGUS MATTHEWS (V.O.)
          . . . So, the truck arrived at
          Menzies Bay with this thing
          already constructed . . .

BACK TO ANGUS

                    ANGUS MATTHEWS
          . . . This is the lengths to
          which people were prepared
          to go.

MAP — Animated white dots trace the path the crew took from Victoria to Menzies Bay.

> NARRATOR (V.O.)
> The convoy of Sealand rescue vehicles drove through the night up Vancouver Island to Menzies Bay, arriving in the early hours of the following morning.

                                    FADE TO:

EXT. MENZIES BAY — DAY

The Sealand crew has attached float lines to the shoreline and several boats have piles of equipment and netting.

PHOTO — Two people in a boat watching the Sealand crew.

> ANGUS MATTHEWS (V.O.)
> There were quite a few people suspicious of what we were up to . . .

BACK TO ANGUS

> ANGUS MATTHEWS
> . . . One guy who really accosted us was a guy by the name of Grant Thompson . . .

EXT. MENZIES BAY — DAY

Grant Thompson looks down at the bay.

WIDER — Grant is on a tug, watching all the activity.

> ANGUS MATTHEWS (V.O.)
> . . . he worked for the mill
> at Menzies Bay . . .

Later, several boats linger in the bay.

ANGLE — More boats arrive at the scene.

> ANGUS MATTHEWS (V.O.)
> . . . I remember him coming
> across in his boat and being
> really aggressive. And then
> Bill Davis . . .

GRANT AND BILL — On the shore near where Miracle was rescued and discussing the events of her rescue.

> ANGUS MATTHEWS (V.O.)
> . . . who he worked with, came
> over and talked to him and
> he, sort he of, understood and
> then he got enthusiastic . . .

The tug comes over to help.

> ANGUS MATTHEWS (V.O.)
> . . . and then he asked if he
> could help . . .

The boats continue to mill around.

> ANGUS MATTHEWS (V.O.)
> . . . And then he turned up
> with a bunch of the fallers,
> that'd all been laid off, they
> brought down for bucking up
> the timbers to build a square
> pen . . .

EXT. MENZIES BAY (2000) — DAY

The deadhead lifting barge on the shoreline
sits almost where it was so many years
before.

> ANGUS MATTHEWS (V.O.)
> . . . They had a barge up on
> shore they used for lifting
> deadheads out of the bay. They
> stuffed that back in the water
> with its A-frame on it . . .

ANGLE — Boom boats arrive to help.

> ANGUS MATTHEWS (V.O.)
> . . . They brought out their
> boom boats. I mean, it was
> just incredible . . .

PHOTO — Miracle with visible scars on her
back.

                    NARRATOR (V.O.)
          The plan was to capture . . .

PHOTO — Miracle surfaces, the scars still
visible.

                    NARRATOR (V.O.)
          . . . Miracle the same way
          Sealand had captured killer
          whales in the past.

EXT. OAK BAY SHORE — DAY

Matthews describes the shape of the pen with
his hands.

                    ANGUS MATTHEWS
          We were able to string what we
          call is a pond net, which is
          sides and a bottom . . .

EXT. MENZIES BAY (AUGUST 1977) — DAY

Sealand workers, using log booms and nets,
create a pond net that is attached to the
shoreline.

PHOTO — One man attaches the net to shore
while another in a boat uses a pole to hold
it in place.

PHOTO — Two boats with two men each hover
outside the net pond.

ANGLE — Bill is in his boat inside the pond.
Miracle swims by.

> ANGUS MATTHEWS (V.O.)
> . . . Then we were able to
> set a net around Miracle, it
> wasn't named at that point,
> and Bill Davis in a big
> circle. The net just hangs on
> the bottom. And as we worked
> the net closer and closer and
> make the area smaller and
> smaller. In theory, you're
> going to be able to really
> force, I suppose, the whale
> into the pond net . . .

Miracle comes up and takes a faint breath.

> ANGUS MATTHEWS
> . . . In this instance,
> though, we noticed anywhere
> you sent Bill Davis, the
> whale followed. So we sent
> Bill . . .

PHOTO — Bill's boat is tied up to a log,
while Sealand pulls a net around Bill and
Miracle.

ANGUS MATTHEWS (V.O.)
. . . into the pond net in
his boat against the far side
of it against the log, and
this whale just followed
along . . .

PHOTO — Bill Davis and Grant Thompson secure
a net along a boom log.

ANGUS MATTHEWS (V.O.)
. . . And we expected several
hours' work to actually catch
her, if you will. And it was
at that moment, it not only
dawned on me but all of us, is
that this whale trusted Bill
Davis . . .

BACK TO MIRACLE — She circles slowly in the
pond.

ANGUS MATTHEWS (V.O.)
. . . so much and this whale
was in such distress, it was
prepared to do absolutely
anything for people that were
trying to help it.

Miracle swims slowly just under the surface.
Then she surfaces. Her breath is very faint.

LARRY MCINERNEY (V.O.)
As I recall, she was sunburnt.
She didn't look healthy . . .

Miracle is hoisted out of the water and onto a flat-deck
truck fitted with a sling. (Photo credit: Bill Davis)

48.

INT. LARRY'S HOUSE — DAY

Larry McInerney is in his den.

LOWER THIRD: Larry McInerney, former Sealand Head Diver.

                    LARRY MCINERNEY
. . . and I was quite
surprised when she, when she
blew. It was really nothing,
and I thought, wow, that's a
pretty small whale.

TWO PHOTOS — Bill leans out of his boat and feeds her. Bill puts his hand on her head.

                  ANGUS MATTHEWS (V.O.)
As long as Bill was up at
her forehead with his hand
actually on the melon in the
forehead region, she seemed to
stay very calm . . .

EXT. MAKESHIFT POND — MOMENTS LATER

Miracle is loaded into the sling. She vocalizes nervously.

                  ANGUS MATTHEWS (V.O.)
. . . And so without actually
having to draw her up into the
net as we called it . . .

PHOTO — Looking down on the sling with Miracle in it.

> ANGUS MATTHEWS (V.O.)
> . . . we were able to put a sling in the water around and underneath her and . . .

BACK TO THE POND — Miracle is being lifted up into the sling.

> ANGUS MATTHEWS (V.O.)
> It was easily probably three, four feet too long for Miracle. It was like wrapping a baby in a blanket.

ANOTHER ANGLE — The team is now on shore by the truck.

PHOTO — Miracle wrapped in the sling lined with a soft sheepskin material.

> NARRATOR (V.O.)
> Once Miracle was out of the water, the small barge crane was towed across the bay to the truck . . .

EXT. OAK BAY BEACH HOTEL (1977) — DAY

A young Bob Wright looks over the Oak Bay Beach Hotel pool.

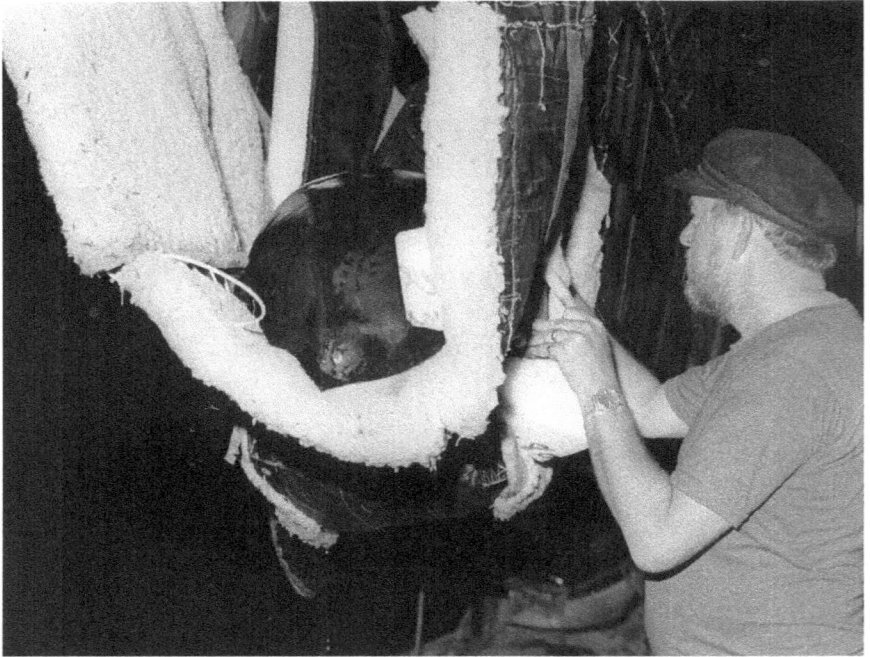

Miracle is made safe and comfortable in a sling. (Photo credit: Bill Davis)

                    NARRATOR (V.O.)
          . . . But Bob Wright had
          another urgent matter to deal
          with before Miracle arrived in
          Victoria.

EXT. OAK BAY BEACH HOTEL — DAY

Establish.

                    BOB WRIGHT (V.O.)
          Beach Hotel came to mind. And
          I knew the owner and I got a
          hold of him and asked if there
          was a possibility that I could
          get some accommodation there
          because I had a VIP coming
          into town . . .

EXT. OAK BAY MARINA (2000) — DAY

                    BOB WRIGHT
          . . . I then informed him that
          I really didn't need a room,
          if he would let us . . .

A SMALL SIGN — Next to the hotel with the
word "pool" and an arrow on it.

EXT. SALTWATER POOL (2000) — DAY

Establish.

            BOB WRIGHT (V.O.)
    . . . have the old saltwater
    swimming pool . . .

The saltwater pool is in rough shape.

            BOB WRIGHT (V.O.)
    . . . and of course, at that
    time he realized we were
    bringing in some sort of an
    animal.

FROM THE SEASIDE — A hose is slung over the
wall and is filling the pool with water.

FROM ABOVE — Pumps and hoses lie across the
rocks.

            ANGUS MATTHEWS (V.O.)
    The pool hadn't been filled
    for years, so Les Wood, the
    manager of the Undersea
    Gardens . . .

BACK TO ANGUS

            ANGUS MATTHEWS
    . . . also owned by Bob
    Wright . . .

UNDERWATER — The old pool is filled with algae
and debris.

                    ANGUS MATTHEWS (V.O.)
          . . . luckily was an ex-Navy
          engineer, and he came over and
          looked at this poor old pool
          and managed to patch the thing
          up to the extent . . .

EXT. POOL SHED — DAY

Les Wood is setting up the pump.

                    ANGUS MATTHEWS (V.O.)
          . . . and get pumps bought and
          installed.

Water trickles out of the leaky old pool and
into the ocean.

                                        FADE TO:

EXT. MENZIES BAY — EVENING

The breeze blows over Menzies Bay. Bill's
boat sits by the shore. Alone and empty.

                    NARRATOR (V.O.)
          While Les Wood and his crew
          worked feverishly preparing
          the pool, the shadows of
          the evening were turning to
          darkness at Menzies Bay . . .

TWO PHOTOS — The crew finish prepping the flat-
deck truck crate.

                    NARRATOR (V.O.)
     . . . And now the Sealand
     crew were looking for a way
     to transfer Miracle from the
     barge crane to the back of the
     flat-deck truck.

BACK TO ANGUS

                    ANGUS MATTHEWS
     Another one of those quirks of
     fate . . .

PHOTO — The land-based A-frame log hoist.

                    ANGUS MATTHEWS (V.O.)
     . . . There's a gigantic
     A-frame hoist that's used for
     lifting logs off . . .

EXT. LOADING AREA (1977) — DAY

The crew tests the log hoist with their
sling.

                    ANGUS MATTHEWS (V.O.)
     . . . logging trucks and
     dumping them in the bay. Grant
     and his guys were able to
     get this thing running and we
     hooked the cable on and they
     hoisted the whale up with
     it . . .

PHOTO — Miracle in the sling in the black of night.

>   ANGUS MATTHEWS (V.O.)
>   . . . Brought it in and
>   lowered her down on the back
>   of the truck.

PHOTO — Miracle in the pond just before being put into the sling.

>   NARRATOR (V.O.)
>   Even with the good fortune
>   of a co-operative whale, log-
>   lifting equipment and skilled
>   manpower . . .

PHOTO — Miracle in the flat-deck truck crate.

>   NARRATOR (V.O.)
>   . . . it was well into night
>   before they were ready to make
>   the trek back to Victoria.

EXT. OLD ISLAND HIGHWAY (AUGUST 1977) — NIGHT

MIRACLE POV — She is travelling down the road in the truck. Trees and street lights zip by.

>   BOB WRIGHT (V.O)
>   We travelled at night . . .

BACK TO BOB WRIGHT

> BOB WRIGHT
> . . . because we wanted to
> keep the animal as cool as
> possible and we wanted to
> go . . .

BACK TO MIRACLE POV — Another tree passes by.

> BOB WRIGHT (V.O.)
> . . . when there was a minimum
> of traffic.

BACK TO LARRY MCINERNEY

> LARRY MCINERNEY
> We pulled into this gas
> station one time, and uh, she
> vocalized, and the attendant
> sort of goes, "What was that?"
> And I think Angus said, "It's
> a killer whale."

BACK TO BOB WRIGHT

> BOB WRIGHT
> You know, kind of looked at
> us like we were a bunch of
> nuts. Let's go up and take a
> look . . .

PHOTO — Les Woods pours water over Miracle to
keep her skin moist.

                    BOB WRIGHT (V.O.)
          I can still remember the look
          on the young lad's face . . .

MAP — Animated red dots start at Menzies Bay
and trace the team's path to Victoria.

MAP — Animated red dots trace Miracle's trip
to Victoria.

                                        FADE TO:

EXT. OAK BAY BEACH HOTEL (1977) — MOMENTS
LATER

Establish.

Birds chirp with the sun rising.

                    NARRATOR (V.O.)
          The unofficial consensus
          amongst Miracle's rescuers
          was that if she was going to
          die . . .

EXT. OAK BAY SHORELINE — MORNING

A quiet overcast morning.

                    NARRATOR (V.O.)
          . . . it would be during
          the six-hour road trip to
          Victoria . . .

EXT. OAK BAY BEACH HOTEL POOL — MINUTES LATER

MIRACLE POV — The truck is backed across the lawn.

> NARRATOR (V.O.)
> . . . But Miracle was still alive and breathing as they backed the truck across the lawn to the outdoor pool.

FADE OUT:

EXT. OAK BAY BEACH HOTEL POOL — MINUTES LATER

Miracle wobbles back and forth, barely floating, covered in white lanolin.

SUPERSCRIPT: August 12, 1977.

ANOTHER ANGLE — Miracle rises slowly to take a breath.

ON HER DORSAL FIN — It's shaky and sticking out of the water. She's covered in lanolin.

> ANGUS MATTHEWS (V.O.)
> And for the first couple of moments, as she swam out of the stretcher we all wondered . . .

EXT. SHORE (2000) — DAY

BACK TO ANGUS

Sealand staff hold Miracle up after putting her in the Oak Bay Beach Hotel pool following her transfer from Menzies Bay. (Photo credit: Peter Termehr)

Miracle is placed on a foam pad so she could rest and be examined by Sealand staff. (Photo credit: Peter Termehr)

Miracle, covered in lanolin, swims slowly around the
Oak Bay Beach Hotel pool. (Photo credit: Peter Termehr)

Miracle slowly gained strength, and after a few days she was able
to swim on her own. (Photo credit: Rochelle Termehr)

                    ANGUS MATTHEWS
          . . . if this trip had been
          too much and if she would, in
          fact, survive . . .

Miracle just moves slowly around the pool.

                    ANGUS MATTHEWS (V.O.)
          . . . It was very obvious that
          we were in serious trouble
          when she was lowered down into
          the pool.

EXT. OAK BAY BEACH HOTEL POOL — MOMENTS LATER

Angus Matthews, Jay Hyman, Allan Hoey and
Larry McInerney grab Miracle and hold her to
the surface. She panics and vocalizes.

                    LARRY MCINERNEY (V.O.)
          She basically just sort of
          sank to the bottom then we
          grabbed her and lifted her up.

                    ANGUS MATTHEWS (V.O.)
          And as we were actually
          holding her . . .

BACK TO ANGUS

                    ANGUS MATTHEWS
          . . . It felt like you could
          feel the life coming right out
          of her.

EXT. SALTWATER POOL (2000) — AFTERNOON

Allan Hoey is sitting on the shoreline next to the saltwater pool.

LOWER THIRD: Dr. Allan Hoey, former head veterinarian, Sealand of the Pacific.

>   DR. ALLAN HOEY
>   Jay Hyman and I grabbed the
>   animal. And . . .

BACK TO THE POOL — They try to lift Miracle up.

>   DR. ALLAN HOEY (V.O.)
>   . . . lifted the animal up
>   to the surface again. Didn't
>   appear to be breathing.

Four of them pull her over to the edge of the pool.

>   DR. ALLAN HOEY (V.O.)
>   Didn't do anything, so we were
>   banging away, kicking and sort
>   of kneeing the animal to try
>   and shake something up to make
>   the animal do something . . .

BACK TO ANGUS

                    ANGUS MATTHEWS
          And with the six or eight of
          us all gathered around holding
          her up, it really looked like
          the story had ended right
          there . . .

EXT. SALTWATER POOL (1977) — MORNING

Angus has his hand on Miracle's foam pad.

                    ANGUS MATTHEWS (V.O.)
          . . . And I remember my back
          aching as we held onto her,
          and we held onto her . . .

ON MIRACLE — Her back is visible.

Allan Hoey looks at the marks on her back. He
rubs her skin with a cloth.

                    ANGUS MATTHEWS (V.O.)
          . . . I actually remember
          standing up thinking it was
          probably all over . . .

BACK TO ANGUS

                    ANGUS MATTHEWS
          . . . This was a, a rock-
          bottom moment.

EXT. OAK BAY BEACH HOTEL POOL — LATER

A crowd is leaning on the fence watching the Sealand group try to save Miracle.

>   DR. ALLAN HOEY (V.O.)
>   All of a sudden she . . .

ON MIRACLE — She is lying on a foam mat.

BACK TO ALLAN

>   DR. ALLAN HOEY
>   . . . took a big breath and
>   everybody else took a big
>   breath . . .

ANGLE — Miracle is covered in lanolin and swims slowly around the pool.

ANOTHER ANGLE — Miracle is still on the foam pad. The lanolin has been cleaned off her skin.

LATER — Miracle is now swimming in the pool with Angus and Larry in the pool watching over her.

>   ANGUS MATTHEWS (V.O.)
>   What followed was a whole day
>   and an entire night, of four
>   of us taking turns, round and
>   round the pool walking her
>   literally. And as we walked
>   we found that, um, she was
>   gradually limbering up . . .

EVEN LATER — Miracle is grabbed by the handlers for a checkup.

EXT. OAK BAY BEACH HOTEL POOL — NIGHT

Miracle is being walked — and make it night/dusk.

> ANGUS MATTHEWS (V.O.)
> . . . gradually able to move her tail a bit more . . .

BACK TO ANGUS

> ANGUS MATTHEWS
> . . . gradually able to swim a bit more for herself, but it was out of the question for her to stay on the surface herself. Had she not been held to the surface . . .

BACK TO THE POOL

Sealand staff pull Miracle onto the foam pad for a checkup.

> ANGUS MATTHEWS (V.O.)
> . . . there is no doubt she would've, would've drowned.

ANGLE — Miracle swims by herself and is looking a bit stronger.

FADE TO:

ON A SIGN — It reads "medical staff only."

EXT. OAK BAY BEACH HOTEL — MORNING

Angus Matthews is on the phone in a makeshift office.

SUPERSCRIPT: The next day.

ON A YOUNGER ALLAN HOEY — He is on the phone.

ON JIM MCBAIN — He is at the side of Miracle's pool.

> ANGUS MATTHEWS (V.O.)
> We had an unusual situation where we had Dr. Allan Hoey, Dr. Jay Hyman, Dr. Tag Gornell, from Seattle, Dr. Jim McBain . . .

Angus and Allan are sitting on the side of the pool with staff milling about.

> ANGUS MATTHEWS (V.O.)
> . . . all working together to formulate an emergency plan. And when we did our first thorough examination of the whale . . .

BACK TO ANGUS

ANGUS MATTHEWS
. . . um, the morning after
she had arrived, that's when
we discovered the seriousness
of her injuries . . .

BACK TO THE POOL

Miracle is moved onto the foam mat.

CLOSER

Allan Hoey, with tweezers and scalpel, cleans
out a large wound on her back just below her
dorsal fin.

ANGUS MATTHEWS (V.O.)
. . . Gunshot wound. We didn't
really realize quite how
serious it was until we really
probed it carefully.

Angus puts his hand on Miracle's back to
reassure her during the wound cleaning and
examination.

BOB WRIGHT (V.O.)
She was very, very lucky.
Because it was obviously
a . . .

BACK TO BOB

A Sealand veterinarian examines the bullet hole
on Miracle's back. (Photo credit: Peter Termehr)

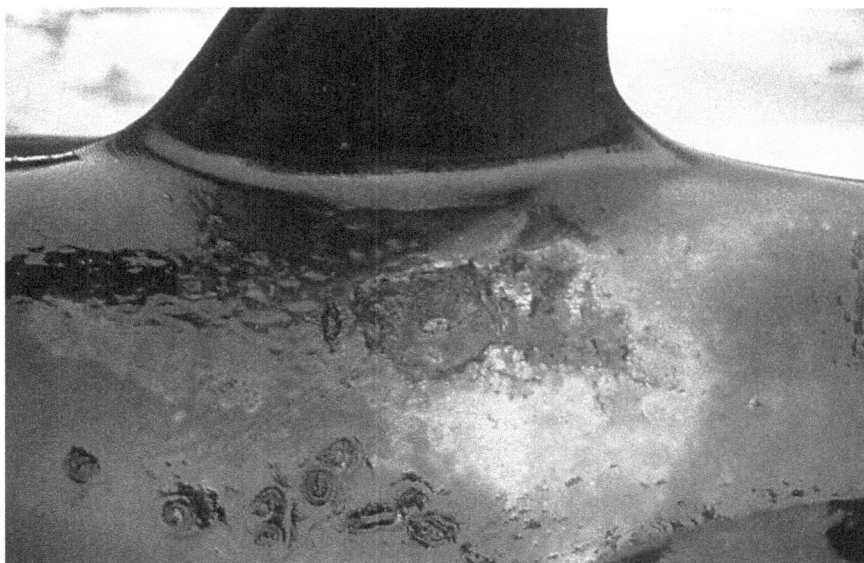

Miracle's scars from the gunshot wound start to heal. (Photo credit: Peter Termehr)

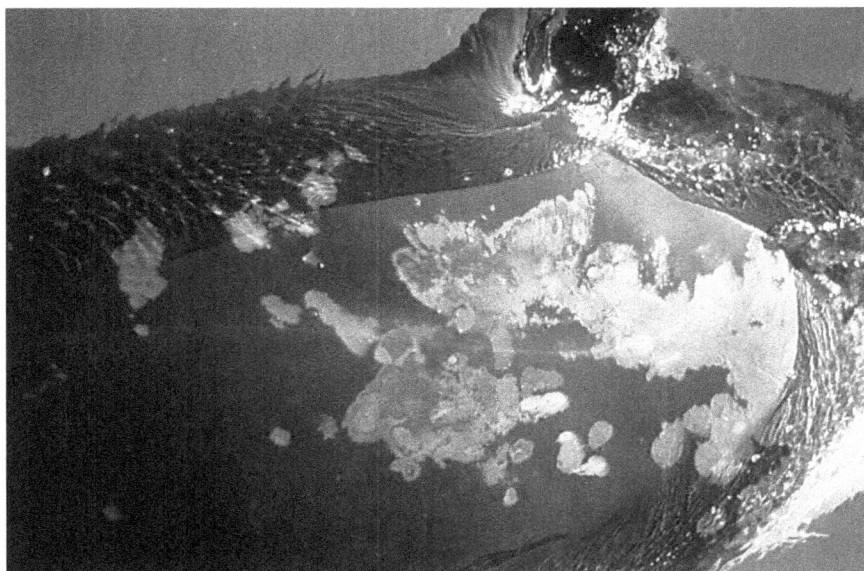

After a month or so, Miracle's wounds are
almost healed. (Photo credit: Rochelle Termehr)

                    BOB WRIGHT
          . . . high-powered rifle, so
          our medical experts had
          determined . . .

Allan examines the entry wound on her back.

                    BOB WRIGHT (V.O.)
          . . . and it went through just
          below her dorsal fin . . .

The group looks at her wound.

                    BOB WRIGHT (V.O.)
          . . . Went in one side and out
          the other and missed any vital
          organs . . .

CLOSE ON ENTRY WOUND

They point at the bullet hole.

                    BOB WRIGHT (V.O.)
          . . . and we did not believe
          that she had even any broken
          ribs. So it was a miracle
          there that a high-calibre
          bullet . . .

BACK TO BOB

                    BOB WRIGHT
          . . . like that did not
          shatter her or tear her apart.

MEDIUM WIDE — Miracle is visible over Dr. Hoey's shoulder.

Allan scrapes out one of Miracle's wounds. It's quite large.

> ANGUS MATTHEWS (V.O.)
> Jay Hyman did some fairly basic surgery to dig into the dorsal fin and actually extract the pieces of the bullet which was later identified as a .303. And it appeared to have come in and hit either cartilage or, or bone tissue at the base of the dorsal fin and then split and . . .

BACK TO ANGUS

> ANGUS MATTHEWS
> . . . actually the exit wounds were what we thought were the entry wounds. They were very large, probably three or four inches across. And the entry wound was actually tiny.

BACK TO MIRACLE

Miracle lies on the foam pad. A handler is gently rubbing her skin with a brush to clean her off.

                    NARRATOR (V.O.)
          The bullet wound on Miracle's
          body was not the only injury
          Miracle sustained . . .

BACK TO ALLAN — He is still working on the
wound.

                    NARRATOR (V.O.)
          . . . The question is, who
          would want to kill a baby
          orca? And why? . . .

CLOSE ON MIRACLE'S BACK — There are three
parallel scars that appear to be teeth marks.
She also has a patch of cross-hatch marks
that look like net marks.

                    NARRATOR (V.O.)
          . . . If we combine the bullet
          wound with the teeth and
          net marks also found on her
          body . . .

UNDERWATER — A whale's POV through a kelp
forest.

                    NARRATOR (V.O.)
          . . . her brush with death
          suggests an encounter that
          was all too common for killer
          whales up until the late
          1970s.
                              FADE TO:

A sign was erected to ask the visiting public to observe quietly and not frighten the ailing baby killer whale. The makeshift pool was shallow and made of concrete. Any sudden movement by Miracle could easily result in more injuries. (Photo credit: Rochelle Termehr).

After a few weeks in the Oak Bay Beach Hotel pool Miracle seems fully recovered and gets playful. (Photo credit: Rochelle Termehr)

INT. OCEAN (ANIMATED) — DAY

A mother and calf swim along.

CLOSER — The whales swim close together.

> LANCE BARRETT-LENNARD (V.O.)
> It is quite conceivable to me
> that Miracle and her group may
> have been . . .

INT. BARRETT-LENNARD'S OFFICE — DAY

Lance Barrett-Lennard, killer whale
researcher and geneticist, University of
British Columbia and Vancouver Aquarium,
Vancouver, Canada, is in his office.

**LOWER THIRD: Dr. Lance Barrett-Lennard,
Killer Whale Geneticist.**

EXT. OCEAN — DAY

A commercial fishing boat is bobbing in the
water.

ANGLE — A net is being released off the back
of the boat.

> LANCE BARRETT-LENNARD (V.O.)
> . . . hunting for salmon
> in the same area that a
> gillnetter or seine fishery was
> going on . . .

ANIMATION — Miracle splits off from her
mother and swims into a gill net.

      LANCE BARRETT-LENNARD (V.O.)
    . . . and became entangled in
    net . . .

ANIMATED MOTHER — She swims toward her baby
to rescue it from the nets.

      LANCE BARRETT-LENNARD (V.O.)
    . . . Generally, killer whales
    are pretty good at avoiding
    nets . . .

TIGHT — The mother whale grabs onto her baby
with her teeth to try to pull it free.

      LANCE BARRETT-LENNARD (V.O.)
    . . . But the fact she was
    a calf probably made her
    much more vulnerable. We've
    noticed . . .

BACK TO LANCE

      LANCE BARRETT-LENNARD
    . . . in the past that the
    animals that do tend to get
    into trouble with things like
    net . . .

TIGHT — Net mesh sloshes back and forth in
the ocean.

>   LANCE BARRETT-LENNARD (V.O.)
>   . . . They are relatively
>   naïve.

EXT. BOAT (RE-ENACTMENT) — DAY

A fisherman has a rifle and points it at the
water. He shoots.

>   NARRATOR (V.O.)
>   But Miracle was found in
>   Menzies Bay . . .

RESUME ANIMATION

A bullet enters the water and hits the mother
whale as she swims by.

>   NARRATOR (V.O.)
>   . . . a long way from
>   known commercial fishing
>   grounds . . .

INT. OCEAN — DAY

Looking up through netting, we see the
fisherman looking down into the water.

>   NARRATOR (V.O.)
>   . . . So was this possible in
>   her case? . . .

INT. OCEAN (ANIMATED) — DAY

A bullet hits Miracle in the back as she
swims away, bleeding.

FADE TO:

MAP — An animated red circle zooms in on Nanaimo Harbour, on the east side of Vancouver Island.

>   NARRATOR (V.O.)
>   . . . The theory that Miracle
>   encountered a commercial
>   fisherman becomes even
>   more plausible when it was
>   discovered that Miracle was
>   seen swimming in Nanaimo
>   Harbour two weeks or so before
>   Bill Davis found her.

PHOTO — A grainy black-and-white photo of a baby orca.

SUPERSCRIPT: July 21, 1977, Nanaimo Harbour, British Columbia.

INT. GRAEME ELLIS'S LAB — DAY

LOWER THIRD: Graeme Ellis, Killer Whale Researcher.

>   GRAEME ELLIS
>   We didn't believe the report.
>   Thought it was probably some
>   other creature, maybe a doll
>   porpoise. It was very unlikely
>   it was a killer whale . . .

TWO PHOTOS — The baby killer whale in the harbour.

                    GRAEME ELLIS (V.O.)
          . . . So we went down there,
          Ian MacAskie, Michael Bigg and
          myself, and . . .

EXT. BOAT — DAY

They motor out into the harbour looking for
the whale.

                    GRAEME ELLIS (V.O.)
          . . . launched the boat, went
          down, and uh, sure enough it
          was . . .

PHOTO — Miracle's back, close up.

                    GRAEME ELLIS (V.O.)
          . . . a . . . a young killer
          whale, a very young one . . .

PHOTO — Miracle in Nanaimo Harbour near an
industrial part of the bay.

                    GRAEME ELLIS (V.O.)
          . . . obviously distressed
          and zipping back and forth
          alongside the side of this
          freighter.

PHOTO — Miracle almost leaping out of the
water.

Miracle swims erratically in Nanaimo Harbour two weeks before
she was found in Menzies Bay. (Photo credit: Graeme Ellis)

Miracle is frantic as she searches for her mother. (Photo credit: Graeme Ellis)

> NARRATOR (V.O.)
> Ellis confirms that the baby
> killer whale . . .

EXT. NANAIMO HARBOUR — DAY

A gloomy day, looking out into the Salish
Sea.

> NARRATOR (V.O.)
> . . . that they saw in Nanaimo
> Harbour was the same one
> Bill Davis found a few weeks
> later . . .

EXT. OCEAN — DAY

A commercial seiner puts out his net.

> NARRATOR (V.O.)
> . . . This, therefore, puts
> Miracle a few hundred
> kilometres south of Menzies
> Bay . . .

INT. OCEAN (ANIMATED) — DAY

Miracle, bleeding, swims along.

> NARRATOR (V.O.)
> . . . and very close to the
> mouth of the Fraser River,
> where commercial fisheries were
> common at the time . . .

MAP — Animated red dots track her path north through the Salish Sea.

> NARRATOR (V.O.)
> . . . So, based on where Miracle was first seen and where she was found . . .

EXT. MENZIES BAY — DAY

A riptide is moving through the Seymour Narrows at the mouth of Menzies Bay.

> NARRATOR (V.O.)
> . . . she must've travelled north, swimming directly into the treacherous Seymour Narrows . . .

TIGHT — The tidal flow looks like the rapids of a massive river.

> NARRATOR (V.O.)
> . . . home of some of the strongest tidal currents in the world . . .

ANIMATED SEYMOUR NARROWS MAP — White arrows show Miracle's path on an ebb tide, pushing Miracle through the Narrows and away from Menzies Bay.

> NARRATOR (V.O.)
> . . . And if Miracle had
> entered the area during an
> ebb tide, she would have been
> swept through the Narrows
> and may never have been seen
> again . . .

BACK TO MAP — The white arrows now show the
flood tide meeting Miracle's path and how she
is pushed into Menzies Bay.

> NARRATOR (V.O.)
> . . . But she likely
> encountered the Narrows
> during a flood tide, and
> because she was weak from her
> injuries . . .

EXT. MENZIES BAY — DAY

Establish the bay from the hill.

> NARRATOR (V.O.)
> . . . she was likely forced to
> turn into the calm waters of
> Menzies Bay . . .

BACK TO PHOTO — Bill reaches down out of his
boat to pet Miracle.

> NARRATOR (V.O.)
> . . . So it really was a
> miracle that Bill Davis found
> her . . .

BACK TO PHOTO — The Sealand crew loads
Miracle into the sling at Menzies Bay.

> NARRATOR (V.O.)
> . . . It was a miracle that
> she survived the rescue
> and six-hour trek to
> Victoria . . .

ANGLE — Miracle swims slowly in Menzies Bay.

> NARRATOR (V.O.)
> . . . It was a miracle she was
> not swept out to sea, never to
> be seen again . . .

EXT. OAK BAY POOL — DAY

Miracle is swimming erratically on her side
in the pool.

> NARRATOR (V.O.)
> . . . But she would need at
> least one more miracle before
> her rescue would be considered
> a success.
>
> FADE TO:

EXT. OAK BAY BEACH HOTEL POOL — DAY

Establish.

SUPERSCRIPT: Mid-August 1977.

OVERLOOKING THE POOL — They've placed a tarp over Miracle to keep the sun off her.

TIGHTER — The crew is moving her onto the foam pad.

> ANGUS MATTHEWS (V.O.)
> Once they had a blood test,
> the vets were able to . . .

The team is making notes and observing and feeding Miracle.

> ANGUS MATTHEWS (V.O.)
> . . . run a whole series of
> analysis and comparisons . . .

They lift Miracle's tail so Allan can take a blood sample from a vein.

> ANGUS MATTHEWS (V.O.)
> . . . Allan always looked at
> something called LDH, which
> determined the level of
> bruising and tissue damage.
> And it was very, very high, as
> you would expect . . .

ANOTHER ANGLE — Angus and Allan hover over Miracle as they take the sample.

WIDER ANGLE — The same procedure is shown.

                    ANGUS MATTHEWS (V.O.)
          . . . Jay Hyman was always
          one that was always watching
          very carefully the white count
          and . . .

BACK TO ANGUS

                    ANGUS MATTHEWS
          . . . we were seeing white
          counts that were the highest
          that ever been seen in any
          killer whale . . .

BACK TO POOL — Miracle swims slowly toward
her foam pad.

                    ANGUS MATTHEWS (V.O.)
          . . . And in this case, the
          white counts were running
          24, 25, even 30 thousand. Um,
          unheard of in any even very
          sick killer whale. Normals
          would run in the 8 to 12
          thousand range . . .

ANGLE — The team pulls Miracle back up onto
the foam pad for another examination.

                    ANGUS MATTHEWS (V.O.)
          . . . And that's when it was
          painfully obvious that we had
          a raging infection . . .

ON POOLSIDE TABLE — An array of white bottles
of vitamins sits on the table. A prescription
bottle and a chart with pills is lined up on
it for Miracle's treatments.

> ANGUS MATTHEWS (V.O.)
> . . . We started banging away
> with antibiotics the first day
> and this involved every four
> hours . . .

ANGLE — Miracle is on the foam pad.

> ANGUS MATTHEWS (V.O.)
> . . . drawing her up out of
> the water onto a mat . . .

ON THE NEEDLE — It sits on the desk next to a
watch.

> ANGUS MATTHEWS (V.O.)
> . . . Um, the needle is a good
> four inches long, and it's
> carefully . . .

Miracle gets an injection of antibiotics.

> ANGUS MATTHEWS (V.O.)
> . . . injected into the back
> and we have to try and move
> injection sites as much as
> possible. And in go the
> antibiotics and it was just a
> matter of . . .

Sealand aquarium staff put Miracle on a foam pad many times so they could examine her wounds. (Photo credit: Tag Gornall)

After giving Miracle the injection they move
her on the foam pad to another part of the
pool.

> ANGUS MATTHEWS (V.O.)
> . . . a race against time as
> to whether the infection would
> win or the antibiotics would
> do the job.

Miracle vocalizes as they shift her around.

> NARRATOR (V.O.)
> After the first few critical
> days and weeks, Sealand staff
> began to believe she was on
> the road to recovery.

FADE TO:

EXT. OAK BAY BEACH HOTEL POOL — LATER

Miracle's condition appears to have improved
and she is now swimming enthusiastically
around the pool and taking fish from Larry
McInerney.

ON A SIGN — "Quiet Please! Baby Killer Whale
Receiving Intensive Care."

Once Miracle recovered from her wounds, she was fed herring by hand by Sealand staff at the Oak Bay Beach Hotel pool. (Photo credit: Peter Termehr)

Miracle enjoys the interaction with her handlers in the Oak Bay Beach Hotel pool. (Photo credit: Peter Termehr)

BACK TO ANGUS

>ANGUS MATTHEWS
>The *Times Colonist,* the local
>newspaper, actually took to
>printing the white count in a
>little box beside the weather
>for a couple of weeks. And
>people learned to . . .

AT THE POOL — The crew and their families
watch over the pool activities.

>ANGUS MATTHEWS (V.O.)
>. . . actually watch the white
>count come up and down like
>the stock market . . .

ANGLE — A large crowd of onlookers press up
against the fence.

>ANGUS MATTHEWS (V.O.)
>. . . It was a level of
>involvement with the community
>that I think that quite
>stunned all of us.

ANOTHER ANGLE — A woman points at Miracle,
and the child she is with watches Miracle's
movements.

BACK TO THE MAT

Miracle is on the mat. They draw blood from her tail. A needle is inserted into a vein on the underside of her tail.

> DR. ALLAN HOEY (V.O.)
> We would come and do our medicals in the morning, pull a lot of blood, see the health status of the animal, send it up to the lab . . .

BACK TO OAK BAY HOTEL ENTRANCE

> DR. ALLAN HOEY (V.O.)
> . . . and we'd go up to the Oak Bay Beach Hotel and have breakfast and . . .

BACK TO ALLAN

> DR. ALLAN HOEY
> . . . wait for the phone call to tell to us what the lab results were . . .

MIRACLE'S DOCTORS — They are meeting with Angus at the side of the hotel pool.

> DR. ALLAN HOEY (V.O.)
> . . . One of the highlights of the breakfast menu was eggs Benedict . . .

ANGLE — The medical team examines Miracle's wound.

A large crowd watches as Sealand staff draw blood
from Miracle's tail. (Photo credit: Peter Termehr)

                    DR. ALLAN HOEY (V.O.)
          . . . And it seemed that
          whenever the crew decided
          that they would have eggs
          Benedict . . .

Allan Hoey and Jim McBain are in the pool and
appear to be discussing the results of the
examination.

                    DR. ALLAN HOEY (V.O.)
          . . . That the blood results
          coming back from the lab were
          bad . . .

PANNING ACROSS — The pool.

The rest of the team is there and the mat is
empty.

                    DR. ALLAN HOEY (V.O.)
          . . . Ah, when we ordered
          something else, the lab
          results seemed better . . .

BACK TO ALLAN

                    DR. ALLAN HOEY
          . . . So it got to a point
          where everybody would refuse
          to eat eggs Benedict . . .

ANGLE — Miracle passes directly under the
camera.

                    DR. ALLAN HOEY (V.O.)
               . . . And I still don't eat
               eggs Benedict today.

                                        FADE TO:

                    NARRATOR (V.O.)
               One day, Bill Davis came to
               see her and her condition
               appeared to suddenly take a
               turn for the worse.

INT. BILL DAVIS HOME — DAY

Bill is in his living room chair.

                    BILL DAVIS
               All of a sudden she started to
               really swim around . . .

BACK TO OAK BAY POOL

A diver in the pool with Miracle looks up at
Bill.

                    BILL DAVIS (V.O.)
               . . . I shook the gate and
               asked the diver, I said,
               "Could you let me in to see
               her?" . . .

ANGLE — Miracle is acting funny in the middle
of the pool.

Bill Davis makes a trip to the Oak Bay Beach Hotel pool to visit Miracle. She remembers Bill and gets so excited Sealand staff think her behaviour is the beginning of a medical emergency. (Photo credit: Bill Davis)

Bill Davis visited Miracle a few times during her stay at the Oak Bay Beach Hotel pool. On this occasion Bill got into the pool with her like her handlers and fed her herring fillets. (Photo credit: Bill Davis)

> BILL DAVIS (V.O.)
> . . . He said, "No, I'm too
> busy right now." And he was
> phoning up Sealand to get
> Angus over, the manager of
> Sealand, to see what's wrong
> with this whale. So it was
> only a couple of minutes
> later that Angus came over
> and he was running down there.
> "Oh, I know what the trouble
> is." . . .

EXT. POOL WALL — DAY

Bill and Angus lean over the edge and Miracle
comes up to Bill. Miracle was just happy to
see him.

> BILL DAVIS (V.O.)
> . . . I talked to her a lot in
> Menzies Bay . . .

ANGLE — Miracle is on her back to let Bill
and Angus scratch her chin. She loves the
attention.

> BILL DAVIS (V.O.)
> . . . and she recognized my
> voice when I was talking to
> this other fellow, and she
> went and freaked out around
> there. The poor diver didn't
> know what was happening.

FADE TO:

Miracle makes a tight turn in the pool. And then she comes up to the edge and looks up.

> NARRATOR (V.O.)
> Miracle's bond with Bill Davis would remain strong . . .

WIDER — Bill is on the petting platform and scratches Miracle. She rolls around in the pool just below him.

> NARRATOR (V.O.)
> . . . And even though Bill's visits were infrequent compared to those of her daily handlers, she always remembered Bill and kept a special place for him in her heart . . .

FADE TO:

ON MIRACLE — A series of shots of Miracle moving quickly underwater in the pool.

> NARRATOR (V.O.)
> . . . Just when it appeared her infections were under control, another crisis hit . . .

EXT. OAK BAY BEACH POOL — LATER

ANGLE — Larry is feeding Miracle herring while standing waist-deep in the pool.

                  NARRATOR (V.O.)
    . . . This time it wasn't
    excitement to see Bill but a
    real crisis.

Miracle grabs another herring.

            ANGUS MATTHEWS (V.O.)
    She had been merrily eating
    whole fish, we seemed to be
    putting weight on. Things
    seemed to be looking better
    and one . . .

BACK TO ANGUS

              ANGUS MATTHEWS
    . . . late afternoon, she
    started swimming . . .

BACK TO MIRACLE

She's hunched over and in pain, swimming on
her side.

            ANGUS MATTHEWS (V.O.)
    . . . really erratically and,
    and uh, actually seemed to be
    in a lot of pain . . .

She's in pain.

>   ANGUS MATTHEWS (V.O.)
>   . . . She was hunched over and
>   would circle around the pool
>   very quickly, then stop and
>   then it looked like she was
>   trying to throw up, it . . .
>   it was very frightening . . .

ANGLE — The team grabs Miracle and pulls her
onto the foam pad. She vocalizes in panic.

>   ANGUS MATTHEWS (V.O.)
>   . . . We got her up onto the
>   foam that we always did the
>   medicals on and . . .

PANNING — Miracle lies on the pad as they
examine her again.

>   ANGUS MATTHEWS (V.O.)
>   . . . it was very obvious that
>   was causing her a great deal
>   of discomfort to her as well.

BACK TO BOB

>   BOB WRIGHT
>   So she couldn't digest bones,
>   so they would impact in there
>   much . . .

BACK TO THE POOL

Five handlers are sliding Miracle onto the
foam pad.

                    BOB WRIGHT (V.O.)
          . . . perhaps like the cat has
          fur balls.

Miracle is now on a mat.

                    ANGUS MATTHEWS (V.O.)
          We were able to run this
          scope down into her stomach,
          and sure enough there was, I
          think, every herring bone that
          she had been fed from the
          beginning . . .

BACK TO ANGUS

                    ANGUS MATTEWS
          . . . of time. In this massive
          blockage in her stomach.

EXT. VITAMIN TABLE — LATER

A handler pulls a herring out of a bucket and
fillets it.

                    NARRATOR (V.O.)
          When the team changed her diet
          to fillets and tried different
          stomach remedies . . .

ANGLE — A handler fillets a herring.

> NARRATOR (V.O.)
> . . . Miracle eventually
> would pass the bones and
> recover . . .

ON LARRY — He's waist-deep in the pool,
feeding Miracle a fillet from a white bucket.

> NARRATOR (V.O.)
> . . . And when it appeared
> Miracle's health troubles were
> behind her . . .

Miracle circles around and gently takes a
fillet from Larry.

> NARRATOR (V.O.)
> . . . discussion about her
> future resulted in a very
> heated and public debate.

                                        FADE TO:

**HEADLINE — "The Victorian: whale campaign
alarms Sealand staff."**

BACK TO BOB

> BOB WRIGHT
> A story of this size and
> interest to people about
> animals . . .

Miracle tries to throw up because her stomach is blocked with herring bones. (Photo credit: Brent Cooke)

Miracle is pulled onto the foam pad so staff can investigate her sudden twists and attempts to vomit. (Photo credit: Rochelle Termehr)

BACK TO THE POOL

> BOB WRIGHT (V.O.)
> . . . of course, brought on
> lots of politics . . .

AT THE POOL

Bob reaches over Angus's shoulder to Miracle, who comes up to nudge his hand with her snout.

> BOB WRIGHT (V.O.)
> . . . I can remember a well-
> known anchor newscaster
> and . . .

BACK TO BOB

> BOB WRIGHT
> . . . he announced with this
> great crowd around him . . .

EXT. OAK BAY POOL — DAY

Angus is being interviewed by a journalist.

> BOB WRIGHT (V.O.)
> . . . while the television
> cameras that were focused in
> on him and Miracle that he and
> his friend . . .

BACK TO BOB

                    BOB WRIGHT
         . . . here, who was the purist,
         were down here to release
         Miracle and lead her back out
         to Mother Nature, where she'd
         come from . . .

OUTSIDE — The viewing fence.

A few people look into the pool.

                    BOB WRIGHT (V.O.)
         . . . Well, I can remember one
         little old lady . . .

EXT. OAK BAY BEACH HOTEL GROUNDS — DAY

A small, older woman confronts the
environmentalist Bruce Bott.

                    UN-NAMED WOMAN
         You just come on the scene and
         think you know it all and you
         want to give a little advice.
         I don't think your advice is
         called for or needed.

The journalist enters with his microphone.

                    BRUCE BOTT
         I'm complimentary . . .

The woman gestures toward Miracle's pool.

                    UN-NAMED WOMAN
          I think she's doing well.
          She's doing as well as they
          possibly can do for her.
          You're not needed here. And
          all this stuff you say about
          all . . .

ON THE POOL

Miracle, oblivious to what is happening a
few metres from her pool, takes a herring
from a handler.

                    UN-NAMED WOMAN (V.O.)
          . . . your scientific
          experiences, that's not
          necessary . . .

BACK ON POOL

Miracle continues feeding.

                    UN-NAMED WOMAN (V.O.)
          . . . This animal has the best
          of attention . . .

WIDER — The view from the seawall side of the
pool.

Dozens of onlookers at the viewing fence
watch Miracle swimming peacefully in the
pool.

FADE TO:

INT. OFFICE — DAY

Paul Watson, founder of the Sea Shepherd society, interjects.

> PAUL WATSON
> Bob Wright wasn't very popular
> with Greenpeace . . .

LOWER THIRD: Captain Paul Watson, Sea Shepherd Society.

A YOUNG BOB WRIGHT — He's at Miracle's pool.

> PAUL WATSON (V.O.)
> . . . at the time and with the
> anti-captivity movement. He
> really couldn't do anything
> right. So what happened . . .

BACK TO PAUL

> PAUL WATSON (V.O.)
> . . . here was that Bob
> Wright found himself in a
> position . . .

HEADLINE — "Wright says . . . Bid to free whale flim flam"

> PAUL WATSON (V.O.)
> . . . where he was now to
> the media, he was a hero and
> that didn't sit well with a
> lot . . .

AT THE POOL — Bill Davis feeds Miracle while standing in the pool.

> PAUL WATSON (V.O.)
> . . . of people who were in
> opposition with the fact that
> Bob Wright had captive orcas.
> This was the dilemma.

Miracle takes another herring fillet from a handler.

> NARRATOR (V.O.)
> Although the anti-captivity
> movement had plenty of
> evidence that whales were
> dying prematurely in
> oceanariums . . .

A YOUNG ANGUS — He's looking over the pool at Miracle.

> NARRATOR (V.O.)
> . . . Sealand explained
> publicly that Miracle might
> not do well on her own in the
> wild.

EXT. OAK BAY BEACH HOTEL POOL — DAY

Angus is being interviewed on the lawn.
Intercut with Miracle swimming and being
attended to in the pool.

> YOUNG ANGUS MATTHEWS
> This animal has a couple of
> little problems that shouldn't
> be overlooked in the whole
> matter, and one is we don't
> believe she was taught to feed
> by her mother. In the course
> of some feeding we did here,
> we've tried her on a couple
> of live fish and she showed
> no interest in trying to
> catch . . .

Miracle continues to take food from Sealand
staff's hands.

> YOUNG ANGUS MATTHEWS (V.O.)
> . . . them and no ability to
> try and catch them. Secondly,
> a killer whale to be on its
> own is very unusual . . .

EXT. OCEAN — DAY

A pod of killer whales swim together in open
ocean water.

                    YOUNG ANGUS MATTHEWS (V.O.)
          . . . They're very social
          animals, they travel in
          tightly knit groups . . .

BACK AT THE POOL — The Sealand team is
examining Miracle on the foam pad.

                    YOUNG ANGUS MATTHEWS (V.O.)
          . . . For a baby to have been
          left behind by a pod is really
          unusual, and we wonder if
          something didn't happen to the
          mother . . .

BACK TO YOUNG ANGUS

                    YOUNG ANGUS MATTHEWS
          . . . And the third factor,
          the serious cuts this animal
          has on her back . . .

ON MIRACLE'S BACK

They look at her scars.

                    YOUNG ANGUS MATTHEWS (V.O.)
          . . . are we believe, is
          caused by propellers, and one
          thing we found working with
          this . . .

BACK TO YOUNG ANGUS

          YOUNG ANGUS MATTHEWS
. . . animal at Menzies Bay
is you would drive out in the
Bay . . .

AT MENZIES BAY — Miracle approaches a boat.

          YOUNG ANGUS MATTHEWS (V.O.)
. . . wondering where she was
to feed her, you'd start your
motor, put it in gear, and two
minutes later, right beside
your propeller, there was this
baby . . .

The journalist raises his microphone to his
mouth.

          JOURNALIST
She'll . . . she'll stay . . .
with you if she wants . . .

Angus smiles.

          YOUNG ANGUS MATTHEWS
I don't know. I don't know.
We have a long way to go as
far as care goes, and if you
want to look at turfing our
baby out, you got a couple of
things coming.

EXT. OAK BAY BEACH HOTEL POOL — DAY

Miracle is swimming enthusiastically. She appears to have grown. She takes a fillet from a handler who pets her as she swims by.

>   NARRATOR (V.O.)
>   While the public debate raged
>   on about whether to free
>   Miracle or not . . .

A young Sealand staffer plays with Miracle at the edge of the pool. A diver gets out of the water and sits on the edge of the pool.

MIRACLE'S POOL POV — People are coming down the path to the fence.

>   NARRATOR (V.O.)
>   . . . Sealand staff made plans
>   to move her from the hotel
>   pool to a new pool at Sealand.

Angus is speaking with staff at the edge of the pool.

ON A HOSE

Hoses from the ocean bring water into the pool. Miracle swims across the pool with barely a flip of her tail.

>   ANGUS MATTHEWS (V.O.)
>   This pool, obviously, she was
>   going to outgrow it very, very
>   quickly . . .

BACK TO ANGUS

> ANGUS MATTHEWS
> . . . She couldn't get proper
> exercise in the pool . . .

Veterinarians Jay Hyman and Allan Hoey
conduct a water quality test.

> ANGUS MATTHEWS (V.O.)
> . . . Ah . . . we were having
> trouble at that point keeping
> the water quality up in the
> pool . . .

BACK TO THE POOL

Miracle takes a fillet from one of the staff.
Angus tosses another fillet in the water for
her to fetch. Then she takes another one
from his hand.

> ANGUS MATTHEWS (V.O.)
> . . . When she wasn't eating
> a great deal it was easy, but
> when she was eating 35 and
> 40 pounds of herring a day,
> of course, that ultimately
> ends up in the pool. The
> whole water quality issue was
> becoming a real concern.

A handler pets Miracle. Then Miracle dives
deep in the pool.

Sealand staff prepare the sling that will be used to move Miracle from the Oak Bay Beach Hotel pool to the new pool at the Sealand aquarium. (Photo credit: Rochelle Termehr)

LOOKING OUT — Dark clouds on the horizon.
Wind. A shot of a storm blowing over the Oak
Bay Beach Hotel pool.

> NARRATOR (V.O.)
> Adding to the water quality
> concerns, a severe storm
> during the fall of 1977
> pounded the walls of the pool
> at high tide with logs and
> debris.

PHOTO — A young Sealand staffer feeds Miracle
from a platform attached to the wall.

PHOTO — Another staffer walks the wall
between the pool and the ocean as storm waves
spill over the wall.

> NARRATOR (V.O.)
> Sealand staff realized that
> the old saltwater pool itself
> would be a hazardous place for
> Miracle during the winter and
> she should be moved as soon as
> possible.
>   FADE OUT:

EXT. SEALAND OF THE PACIFIC — DAY

Establish.

MOVING OFF — The sign at the entrance to
Sealand's main building.

ON THE NEW POOL — Men are looking over the new pool and appear to be deep in conversation.

> NARRATOR (V.O.)
> After two months of construction, the new pool was ready for Miracle. The question now facing Sealand was not so much when to move her, but how.

BACK TO ANGUS

> ANGUS MATTHEWS
> The options were fairly straightforward. We could bring a crane down . . .

PHOTO — Miracle is lifted out of the water at Menzies Bay.

> ANGUS MATTHEWS
> . . . and lift her out onto a truck . . .

EXT. STREET — DAY

Establish the street entrance to the marina and Sealand.

> ANGUS MATTHEWS (V.O.)
> . . . And take her over to the nearby marina, and another crane, reach her down and put her in the new pool . . .

Peter Termehr films Miracle in the sling held up by a scaffold structure at the Oak Bay Beach Hotel pool. (Photo credit: Rochelle Termehr)

IN THE PARKING LOT

Men are discussing the logistics of the move.

> ANGUS MATTHEWS (V.O.)
> . . . That whole process would
> take two to three hours at
> least and . . .

EXT. MENZIES BAY (AUGUST 1977) — AFTERNOON

The Sealand team is loading Miracle into the
sling.

> ANGUS MATTHEWS (V.O.)
> . . . we had such a terrible
> experience moving her the first
> time . . .

BACK TO ANGUS

> ANGUS MATTHEWS
> . . . We really wanted to try
> and minimize the move time as
> much as possible . . .

EXT. OAK BAY BEACH HOTEL POOL (1977) — DAY

Miracle swims slowly around the pool. The
ocean is just behind the wall next to it.

> ANGUS MATTHEWS (V.O.)
> . . . Second option was to
> bring in a barge in right
> beside the pool at high tide
> and reach over with a crane
> and pick her up and put her on
> the barge, take her and load
> her in, and lower her in from
> the back of the new pool.

FADE TO:

BACK TO BOB

> BOB WRIGHT (V.O.)
> How do you move a killer
> whale from her intensive care
> unit . . .

ANIMATED AERIAL PHOTO — Shows the location of
the Oak Bay Beach Hotel with a red circle.

PAN DOWN — The location of Sealand of the
Pacific is shown, then a red circle appears
and is labelled "Miracle's New Pool."

> BOB WRIGHT (V.O.)
> . . . to her new home, which
> was only perhaps four blocks
> apart? And do it safely . . .

BACK TO OAK BAY POOL — Much of the water has
been drained out of the pool. A huge crowd
looks through the fence.

>   BOB WRIGHT (V.O.)
>   . . . And we knew there would
>   be literally . . .

ANGLE — A crowd lines up at Sealand's
entrance.

>   BOB WRIGHT (V.O.)
>   . . . thousands of people
>   out there when this came to
>   pass . . .

BACK TO BOB

>   BOB WRIGHT
>   . . . I guess faint heart
>   never kissed a fair lady . . .

BACK TO OAK BAY POOL

Scaffolding has been constructed on the edge
of Miracle's pool. Cameraman Peter Termehr is
perched up high to film Miracle being loaded
in a sling.

>   BOB WRIGHT (V.O.)
>   . . . and so we decided to
>   move her by helicopter . . .

PHOTO — Miracle's sling lies on the ground.

>   BOB WRIGHT (V.O.)
>   . . . which up had, up to that
>   time, had never been done
>   before.

PHOTO — Photographer Peter Termehr sits on the scaffolding, ready to film the event.

EXT. OAK BAY BEACH HOTEL POOL — LATER

Workers carry in pipes and the sling.

BACK TO ANGUS

> ANGUS MATTHEWS (V.O.)
> Now, it's outrageous to think
> of flying a killer whale. No
> one had ever done it before.
> But, you know, if you're . . .

BACK TO OAK BAY POOL — Workers are hooking up the cables that will hold the sling.

> ANGUS MATTHEWS (V.O.)
> . . . a killer whale, once
> you are out of the water, who
> really cares whether you're
> on a truck or flying. It makes
> a big difference, I suppose,
> to people, but for a killer
> whale to be out of the water
> at all is such an abnormal
> experience . . .

FROM THE OAK BAY HOTEL — Overlooking the pool and scaffolding structure of Miracle's pool.

TIGHTER — Everyone is gathered around and under the structure.

PHOTO — A still of the orange helicopter on the ground.

The sling is carried into the pool.

> ANGUS MATTHEWS (V.O.)
> On the selected day in
> February, a large scaffold
> structure was built in the
> pool and Miracle was loaded
> this time into a custom-fitted
> sling.

The men pull Miracle into the sling. She vocalizes in fear.

BACK TO ALLAN

> DR. ALLAN HOEY
> We knew, because we had moved
> animals before . . .

Miracle is now loaded in the sling and the cables are hooked up.

> DR. ALLAN HOEY (V.O.)
> . . . that the slings worked
> well, and everything was fine
> in that regard . . .

ANGLE — A white sheet is tested as a cover to put over Miracle while she is travelling in the sling.

Sealand staff lay out the foam lining used in the sling that will transport Miracle to her new pool at Sealand a few blocks away. (Photo credit: Rochelle Termehr)

Miracle is loaded into the sling. (Photo credit: Rochelle Termehr)

                    DR. ALLAN HOEY (V.O.)
          . . . We knew that it was
          a matter of getting that
          helicopter hook up . . .

They check the steel bar and eye loop that
will take the helicopter hook.

                    DR. ALLAN HOEY (V.O.)
          . . . lifting that animal . . .

TIGHT — Miracle's head is in the sling. She
is still.

                    DR. ALLAN HOEY (V.O.)
          . . . Virtually all animals
          that had been transported in
          slings get quiet . . .

WIDER — They slide a piece of foam rubber
into the sling beside her.

                    DR. ALLAN HOEY (V.O.)
          . . . and they stay in the
          sling, and that's not a
          problem, so we had that going
          for us . . .

Angus looks down at Miracle's positioning in
the sling.

          DR. ALLAN HOEY (V.O.)
. . . Our concern was that
somewhere along the line the
animal would squirm . . .

After Allan waves his arm, they reposition
Miracle a bit.

          DR. ALLAN HOEY (V.O.)
. . . and do something and
slip out of the sling . . .

Allan Hoey watches the crew load the whale.

          DR. ALLAN HOEY (V.O.)
. . . But we had a crew of
divers that were in the boat
and they were going underneath
in the event that that
happened . . .

They let Miracle out of the sling and test it
again.

          DR. ALLAN HOEY (V.O.)
. . . The word from Bob was
that if the helicopter and the
whale go down, save the whale,
worry about the helicopter
afterwards.

EXT. SEALAND PARKING LOT — DAY

The helicopter is standing by with its rotor
blades running.

DR. ALLAN HOEY (V.O.)
We found out later, of course,
that the helicopter crew said
if anything goes wrong, drop
the whale . . .

BACK TO ALLAN

DR. ALLAN HOEY
. . . So everybody was looking
after themselves.

FADE TO:

EXT. SEALAND PARKING LOT — DAY

The helicopter takes off. The cable for
lifting Miracle is dragging on the ground.

TIGHTER — On the cable.

ANGUS MATTHEWS (V.O.)
When the helicopter came in,
we had gone through the drill
and practised this several
times. We knew what was
happening, but nobody had told
Bob Wright. The helicopter
was to ground the static
charge before it picks up the
whale . . .

BACK TO ANGUS

> ANGUS MATTHEWS
> . . . otherwise it goes
> through the whale and us and
> the divers in the pool. So,
> with the hook hanging down
> from the helicopter . . .

The helicopter hovers above the pool.

> ANGUS MATTHEWS (V.O.)
> . . . it came in about 25 to
> 30 feet from the pool and
> started banging the hook . . .

LOOKING UP — The helicopter hovers overhead.

> ANGUS MATTHEWS (V.O.)
> . . . around on the rocks. Of
> course, poor Bob never thought
> this was a great idea from the
> outset was . . .

FROM THE OCEAN'S EDGE — The scaffold
structure and handlers are silhouetted in the
morning sun.

> ANGUS MATTHEWS (V.O.)
> . . . who was, frankly, much
> more attached to his animals
> than he wanted to really
> admit, I think . . .

BACK TO ANGUS

> ANGUS MATTHEWS
> . . . Bob was sort of yelling,
> "Over here! Over here!" We
> knew that they were grounding
> out the static charge . . .

The hook comes down and they put it through the loop.

> ANGUS MATTHEWS (V.O.)
> . . . brought the hook over,
> hooked on . . .

At first, all we can see is the top of the sling moving away from the scaffold.

> ANGUS MATTHEWS (V.O.)
> . . . lifted up and . . .

PANNING DOWN — Miracle is now hovering over her old pool. Handlers guide the slide with ropes so that she doesn't bump into anything during takeoff.

PHOTO — Miracle is in the sling just above the height of the scaffold structure.

> ANGUS MATTHEWS (V.O.)
> . . . I never thought I'd see
> the day that I would see a
> flying killer whale but that's
> exactly what happened.

Miracle takes flight from the scaffolding structure set up at the Oak Bay Beach Hotel pool and is flown across the water to Sealand. (Photo credit: Rochelle Termehr)

UPWARDS — The sling twirls slowly in the wind after the men let go of the guide ropes.

WIDER — The helicopter flies across the blue sky, with Miracle hanging below in the sling.

EXT. SEALAND OF THE PACIFIC — MOMENTS LATER

A huge crowd runs across the Sealand parking lot, trying to get a closer look at the flying killer whale.

PHOTO — Miracle in the sling, just above the walls of Sealand.

RESUME — The sling is lowered into the hands of waiting Sealand staff who guide it over the water of Miracle's new pool.

ANGLE — A man flags the helicopter to come down a little more.

ANOTHER ANGLE — Wind from the helicopter whips the water in the pool, the hair and clothing of the handlers. It's a tense moment. Then,

ANOTHER ANGLE — Three men sit in a small punt in the pool and wedge Miracle's sling between them and the wharf.

Miracle stayed quite still during her flight. This was the first time that a killer whale had been moved by helicopter anywhere in the world. Even with weeks of preparation, there was a lot of concern that she would somehow squirm out of the sling while in transit. It was a very anxious moment for everyone involved in the operation. (Photo credit: Rochelle Termehr)

Miracle hangs under the helicopter in a sling. She seems tiny compared to the helicopter. (Photo credit: Rochelle Termehr)

Miracle comes in to land at her new pool at Sealand. (Photo credit: Rochelle Termehr)

They quickly untie the cover over Miracle so she will release from the sling once it's in the water. A few moments later . . .

DIVERS — They scramble to pull the rest of the sling under Miracle while keeping her afloat so she can breathe.

> BILL DAVIS (V.O.)
> They lifted her up with a helicopter and flew her the quarter of a mile from there to Sealand and her new pool and she was very upset about that . . .

ANGLE — The punt backs away, and Miracle frantically swims out of the sling. She is scared and vocalizing.

INT. MIRACLE'S NEW POOL — CONTINUOUS

It's a dark, deep pool, vastly different from her shallow pool at the Oak Bay Beach Hotel. She's hovering by the side of it.

> BILL DAVIS (V.O.)
> It took her quite a while to get over that experience.

A Sealand staffer reaches over the side to console her.

> NARRATOR (V.O.)
> Miracle's new home must have
> seemed like a bottomless pit
> compared to the small recovery
> pool that had become so
> familiar . . .

ON MIRACLE — She thrashes away in the water,
fearful and obviously in distress.

> NARRATOR (V.O.)
> . . . She panicked and swam
> erratically, vocalizing in
> terror.

ANGLE — Bill stands with other staff, looking
down at Miracle.

Miracle tries to get out of the pool and
crawl up onto the catwalk.

> BILL DAVIS (V.O.)
> I went in with her. Yeah, she
> was very upset . . .

BACK TO BILL

> BILL DAVIS
> . . . And she wouldn't eat for
> a few days . . .

RESUME THE NEW POOL — Bill is at the edge of
the pool, talking to her.

> BILL DAVIS (V.O.)
> . . . and I went in, helped
> entice her to get back on her
> feeding again . . .

ON A LOWER PLATFORM — Bill is able to reach down and scratch Miracle's belly.

> BILL DAVIS (V.O.)
> It wasn't very long before
> she came out of it. I think
> she was in some kind of
> shock . . .

ANOTHER SHOT — Miracle pokes her head out of the water and Bill rubs her chin.

> BILL DAVIS (V.O.)
> . . . for a while with the
> helicopter and so many people
> around her.
>
> FADE OUT:

FADE IN:

EXT. SEALAND ENTRANCE — DAY

A SIGN SAYS: "WELCOME TO Sealand — CONTINUOUS SHOWS."

> NARRATOR (V.O.)
> Miracle not only adjusted to
> her new pen at Sealand . . .

TWO PHOTOS — First, Miracle rises up to grab a herring a Sealand staffer is holding between his teeth. Then she leaps up and grabs one from his hand, 10 feet above the water.

> NARRATOR (V.O.)
> . . . she went on to become a star performer. People came in droves to see what appeared to be a complete success story . . .

ANGLE — Miracle does a dolphin jump in the middle of the pool. Then she leaps up to touch a white foam stick and finally does a spectacular back flip.

FADE TO:

EXT. MIRACLE'S POOL — LATER

The facility is closed and Miracle is by herself in the pool. No audience, no handlers. She pokes her head out of the pool, looking to see if anyone is around.

HEADLINE — "IS MIRACLE A MISFIT? SEALAND."

> NARRATOR (V.O.)
> . . . But as time went by . . .

BACK TO MIRACLE — She is alone and floating on her back.

Miracle leaps up to touch a ball during a performance. (Photo credit: Bill Davis)

Miracle practises her routine with a trainer. (Photo credit: Peter Termehr)

Miracle dunks a ball into a basketball net while performing
at Sealand of the Pacific. (Photo credit: Rochelle Termehr)

>   NARRATOR (V.O.)
> . . . Miracle's behaviour
> changed and Sealand staff
> began to wonder if Miracle was
> mentally unstable.

PHOTO — Miracle is in a corner of her pool
and rubbing her head against the float.

>   ALEXANDRA MORTON (V.O.)
> She would come and lie right
> beside me at the front of my
> tent . . .

INT. VANCOUVER AQUARIUM LAB — MORNING

Alexandra Morton, a killer whale researcher
from the Raincoast Research Society, is
visiting the scientists at the facility.

>   ALEXANDRA MORTON
> . . . And because she was
> right there and she was a
> baby . . .

BACK TO MIRACLE'S POOL — A young woman
scratches Miracle's back.

>   ALEXANDRA MORTON (V.O.)
> . . . I would reach out and
> start scratching her . . .

PHOTO — Miracle is on her side with her head
in the corner.

Miracle would often retreat to a corner of her Oak Bay Beach Hotel pool and bang her head on the concrete wall. (Photo credit: Rochelle Termehr)

Miracle would continue the behaviour of banging her head after she was transferred to her new pool at Sealand. There she would turn on her side and bang her head on the float. It is believed that she was mimicking a nursing behaviour because she was separated from her mother while still nursing. (Photo credit: Dr. Allan Hoey)

PHOTO — Miracle performing.

> ALEXANDRA MORTON (V.O.)
> . . . As soon as I withdrew my
> hand, she would start banging
> her head at the bottom of
> the float. And I noticed this
> during the day too . . .

IN THE POOL — Miracle is banging her head
against the dock.

> ALEXANDRA MORTON (V.O.)
> When the show was over, she
> would go over to the same
> spot and start banging her
> head . . .

BACK TO ALEXANDRA — She touches Miracle's
forehead.

> ALEXANDRA MORTON
> . . . A matter of fact, her
> whole head in the melon area
> was grey and rough and the
> skin was peeling off of it.

BACK TO MIRACLE'S POOL — The right side of
Miracle's head is visible from above and is
all grey.

UNDERWATER — Miracle swims up to the surface.

> NARRATOR (V.O.)
> Miracle also began to
> get rough with Sealand's
> divers . . .

Miracle dives deeper in the pool.

> LARRY MCINERNEY (V.O.)
> The whale went above him, came
> straight down and bit him on
> the head . . .

A diver loses his regulator, releases
bubbles. He swims for the surface.

> LARRY MCINERNEY (V.O.)
> . . . And actually took his
> hood off, took his mask off.
> At that point he just panicked
> and started heading for the
> surface . . .

The diver looks panicky and doesn't quite get
to the surface.

> LARRY MCINERNEY (V.O.)
> . . . And then Miracle, what
> she did was she bit him on the
> foot, thinking that I'm going
> to get a flipper . . .

The diver's flipper disappears from the frame.

> LARRY MCINERNEY (V.O.)
> . . . but she didn't get the
> foot with the flipper, she got
> the foot with no flipper . . .

PHOTO — Miracle does a spy hop in the pool.

> LARRY MCINERNEY (V.O.)
> . . . Luckily she let go.
> Because we had to take him to
> the hospital . . .

PHOTO — Miracle is underwater with a diver's
leg in frame and some of his diving gear
floating on the surface.

BACK TO LARRY

> LARRY MCINERNEY
> . . . And he had a sprained
> ankle. I thought it was broken
> for a while.

IN THE POOL — Miracle circles around a diver.

FADE OUT:

EXT. INSTITUTE OF OCEAN SCIENCES — DAY

Establish.

                    NARRATOR (V.O.)
          Was Miracle suffering from
          a mental disorder? And what
          could be the cause of her
          unusual behaviours? To find
          out if Miracle may have had a
          chemical imbalance . . .

INT. OCEAN SCIENCES LAB — LATER

Dr. Peter Ross, Marine Mammal Toxicologist,
Institute of Ocean Sciences, Sidney, British
Columbia, Canada, enters the lab.

                    NARRATOR (V.O.)
          . . . we went to see marine
          mammal toxicologist Dr. Peter
          Ross.

INT. DR. PETER ROSS'S LAB — DAY

We follow Dr. Peter Ross into his lab, where
he prepares a sample of blubber.

INT. DR. PETER ROSS'S OFFICE — MOMENTS LATER

**LOWER THIRD: Dr. Peter Ross, Marine Mammal
Toxicologist.**

                    DR. PETER ROSS
          If we look at killer whales,
          we have different populations
          in British Columbia . . .

EXT. OCEAN — DAY

A pod of Northern Resident killer whales
moves across the ocean. . . .

ANGLE — A pod of Southern Resident killer
whales.

> DR. PETER ROSS (V.O.)
> If we look at the three
> populations we studied, the
> Northern Residents, the
> Southern Residents, both of
> which consume fish . . .

ANOTHER ANGLE — The pod comes to the surface
for a breath.

> DR. PETER ROSS (V.O.)
> . . . and the Transients,
> that consume marine mammals.
> Both the Southern Residents
> and the Transient killer
> whale populations were more
> contaminated . . .

BACK TO PETER

> DR. PETER ROSS
> . . . than the endangered
> beluga whale populations in
> the St. Lawrence . . .

A wild killer whale rises up through an almost perfectly still ocean and sends a magnificent breath into the air.

> DR. PETER ROSS (V.O.)
> . . . If the endocrine system is not working as it should be, then we might expect . . .

Another killer whale surfaces through a kelp forest.

> DR. PETER ROSS (V.O.)
> . . . a number of different effects such as malformations and developmental abnormalities.

INT. LANCE BARRETT-LENNARD'S LAB — DAY

Lance is preparing a DNA test using one of Miracle's bones.

> NARRATOR (V.O.)
> But was Miracle from one of the most polluted sub-populations off the Pacific coast?

ANGLE — Gloved hands place samples into test tubes.

WIDER — Barrett-Lennard and Allyson Miscampbell prepping their sample to test Miracle's lineage.

INT. LANCE BARRETT-LENNARD OFFICE — DAY

Lance is at his desk.

>   DR. LANCE BARRETT-LENNARD
>   The reason we were not
>   comfortable with the
>   preliminary . . .

BACK TO LANCE

LOWER THIRD: Dr. Lance Barrett-Lennard, Killer Whale Geneticist, University of British Columbia.

>   DR. LANCE BARRETT-LENNARD
>   . . . result that she was a
>   Transient killer whale, I
>   think Graeme Ellis deserves
>   a lot of the credit for
>   that . . .

INT. GRAEME ELLIS'S OFFICE — DAY

Graeme looks into his microscope.

>   DR. LANCE BARRETT-LENNARD (V.O.)
>   . . . Graeme being someone
>   that actually that worked with
>   Miracle and had known Miracle
>   when she was alive . . .

ANGLE — Graeme holds a film strip up to the window to examine the photos he took in the field.

                DR. LANCE BARRETT-LENNARD (V.O.)
                . . . Graeme was pretty sure
                she was a Resident . . .

CLOSE — Miracle is at Sealand.

                DR. LANCE BARRETT-LENNARD (V.O.)
                . . . killer whale based
                on her behaviour and her
                appearance . . .

PHOTO — Miracle's saddle patch. There's a
black line on it.

                DR. LANCE BARRETT-LENNARD (V.O.)
                . . . But, uh, in particular,
                Miracle had a black line in
                her saddle white patch . . .

BACK TO LANCE

                DR. LANCE BARRETT-LENNARD
                . . . and that's something
                characteristic that we see
                in quite a lot of Residents
                and virtually never see in
                Transients . . .

BACK TO THE LAB — Lance's hands are seen
putting a sample in a gel bath.

Lance pulls out the gel.

> DR. LANCE BARRETT-LENNARD (V.O.)
> . . . So, Graeme was keen for
> me to go back and resample
> Miracle's skeleton . . .

INT. ROYAL BC MUSEUM — DAY

Miracle's skull and teeth lie on a black
cloth on display at the Royal BC Museum.

> DR. LANCE BARRETT-LENNARD (V.O.)
> . . . This time we went back
> and took some bone from the
> skeleton at the Royal BC
> Museum . . .

AT THE GENETICS LAB — The samples are loaded
by Allyson Miscampbell.

> DR. LANCE BARRETT-LENNARD (V.O.)
> . . . And then my friend
> Allyson Miscampbell did . . .

WIDER — Miscampbell pushing the button to
start the test.

> DR. LANCE BARRETT-LENNARY (V.O.)
> . . . the DNA analysis on
> that . . .

OVER LANCE'S SHOULDER — He is pointing at the
result displayed as a photo in a binder.

> DR. LANCE BARRETT-LENNARD (V.O.)
> . . . And this second sample
> it was very clear, it really
> did come from a member of the
> Southern . . .

BACK TO LANCE

> DR. LANCE BARRETT-LENNARD
> . . . Resident killer whale
> community, not a Transient.

FADE TO:

EXT. OCEAN — DAY

A pod of killer whales hunt along a
magnificent shoreline.

ANGLE — A mother surfaces with her calf.

INT. DR. PETER ROSS LAB — DAY

> DR. PETER ROSS (V.O.)
> We might be most worried about
> the first calf or, for that
> matter, any calf. Females
> are . . .

BACK TO PETER

> DR. PETER ROSS
> . . . transferring a high
> concentration of chemicals
> through their milk to their
> offspring.

THREE PHOTOS — First, Miracle knocks a ball out of the pool onto the deck. Second, she catches a herring. Third, she pokes her head out of the water.

> NARRATOR (V.O.)
> But was Miracle's abnormal
> behaviour linked to a
> potential toxic load of
> chemicals, or was there
> a simpler explanation of
> the head banging and the
> aggressive behaviour?

PHOTO — Miracle leaps high into the air.

PANNING UP — From her tail to the tip of her nose.

INT. VANCOUVER AQUARIUM LAB — DAY

Alexandra sits in the lab and shares her theory about Miracle's constant head banging.

> ALEXANDRA MORTON (V.O.)
> Then I went to a conference
> and they showed a film . . .

BACK TO ALEXANDRA

                    ALEXANDRA MORTON
          . . . of a killer whale
          that had been born at an
          oceanarium in the States. And
          I noticed that when the baby
          first approached the mom to
          nurse it would bang its head
          right below where the milk
          was supposed to come out. And
          I guess that was part of the
          letdown response for the milk
          in the mother and that would
          begin the nursing.
                                    FADE TO:

INT. OAK BAY BEACH HOTEL POOL — DAY

A diver is working at the bottom of the pool.

BACK TO ANGUS

                    ANGUS MATTHEWS
          I mean, we knew this animal
          was young but it wasn't really
          'til . . .

They put a towel in Miracle's mouth to look
at her teeth.

                    ANGUS MATTHEWS (V.O.)
          . . . we looked closely
          and realized that she was
          actually missing some of her
          front teeth, several of them
          actually . . .

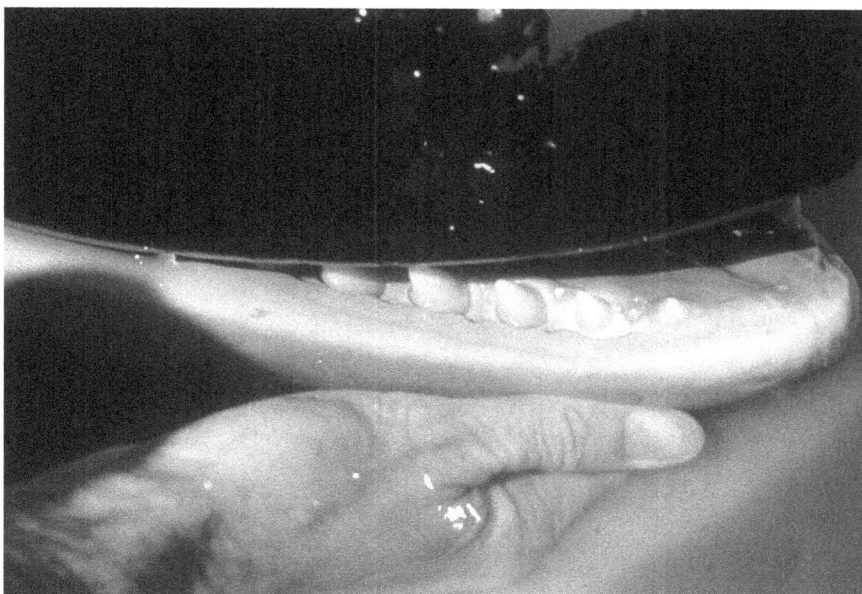

Miracle was so young when she was rescued that she didn't have a full set of teeth. The Sealand staff realized later that she was likely still nursing when she became separated from her mother. (Photo credit: Dr. Allan Hoey)

PHOTO — Miracle has no teeth at the front of her mouth.

> ANGUS MATTHEWS (V.O.)
> . . . we realized that this animal had probably never been weaned. And still should have been nursing with its mother . . .

Allan Hoey gives Miracle a herring.

> ANGUS MATTHEWS (V.O.)
> . . . We started thinking it was about a year old, and before long, we decided, well, maybe seven months, six months. I don't think we ever really established how old it was . . .

A diver plays with Miracle in the pool.

> ANGUS MATTHEWS (V.O.)
> . . . but it was certainly younger than any killer whale that any of the veterinarians had ever worked with and any killer whale that . . .

BACK TO ANGUS

> ANGUS MATTHEWS
> . . . had ever been in any aquarium at that point . . .

BACK TO MIRACLE — She's banging her head
against the side of the pool.

> NARRATOR (V.O.)
> Miracle's head banging, it
> would seem, was similar to
> other odd mammal . . .

PHOTO — Miracle lies against the side of the
pool with her melon touching the wall.

> NARRATOR (V.O.)
> . . . behaviours caused by a
> baby being weaned too soon
> from their mother . . .

TWO PHOTOS — First, Miracle bites a diver's
leg. Then, she approaches another one.

> NARRATOR (V.O.)
> . . . but her violent
> behaviour toward divers
> might've been the remnant of
> another instinct.
>
> DISSOLVE TO:

PHOTO — Looking deep into the pool. Miracle
is a shadow in the deep green water.

ANOTHER PHOTO — Miracle makes a strange face
and curls her tongue.

> LARRY MCINERNEY (V.O.)
> As time went on . . .

EXT. MIRACLE'S SEALAND POOL — DAY

Miracle is aggressively pushing a diver
across the pool.

> LARRY MCINERNEY (V.O.)
> . . . she got more and more
> aggressive, to the point where
> if you were in there for 15
> minutes . . .

UNDERWATER — Miracle slowly swims on her
side.

> LARRY MCINERNEY (V.O.)
> . . . the first five minutes she
> would stay away, the next five
> minutes she would be coming
> closer . . .

BACK TO LARRY

> LARRY MCINERNEY
> . . . the next five minutes
> you would be defending
> yourself . . .

BACK TO THE POOL

Miracle circles around like she's coming back
to a diver.

She swims by on the surface. A white stick
enters the frame for a moment.

Miracle became increasingly aggressive with Sealand's divers who sometimes got into the pool with her to do maintenance. It was later discovered that this behaviour matched similar behaviour seen in Southern Resident Killer whales. (Photo credit: Brent Cooke)

Miracle pushes a diver toward the side of the pool. (Photo credit: Brent Cooke)

>   LARRY MCINERNEY (V.O.)
>   . . . What they did was, they
>   trained her to stay away
>   from a white pole I used to
>   carry . . .

TWO PHOTOS — A handler points at Miracle with
the white stick.

>   LARRY MCINERNEY (V.O.)
>   . . . and that used to help
>   a lot. The procedure used to
>   be . . .

BACK TO LARRY

>   LARRY MCINERNEY (V.O.)
>   . . . there were three divers.
>   I would be working on the
>   chain-link fence with another
>   diver . . .

Miracle hovers near the handler with the
white stick, but out of reach. A diver works
on the pool.

>   LARRY MCINERNEY (V.O.)
>   . . . and the other guy would
>   protect us with the white
>   stick.

BACK TO ALEXANDRA

                    ALEXANDRA MORTON
          But Miracle, very interesting
          response. The first thing she
          did . . .

UNDERWATER — A diver in distress glances back
and forth.

                    ALEXANDRA MORTON (V.O.)
          . . . was pull off their fins
          and then their gloves.

ANGLE — Another diver releases a full breath
of bubbles.

                    ALEXANDRA MORTON (V.O.)
          She basically . . .

PHOTO — Miracle underwater, looking up to her
reaching the surface with something in her
mouth.

                    ALEXANDRA MORTON (V.O.)
          . . . immobilized them . . .

Miracle swims past in the murky green water.

                    ALEXANDRA MORTON (V.O.)
          . . . If you were trying to
          attack, say, a sea lion or
          something . . .

TWO PHOTOS — Panning down Miracle with her
mouth open and teeth showing. Then, she's
looking up with her mouth open.

> ALEXANDRA MORTON (V.O.)
> . . . or any predator
> attacking a prey, the first
> thing you want to do is get
> rid of the things they use to
> get away from you with.

EXT. OAK BAY BEACH HOTEL POOL — DAY

Miracle swims across the pool.

> NARRATOR (V.O.)
> As a Southern Resident killer
> whale, Miracle was genetically
> programmed to prey on salmon
> and not on mammals . . .

EXT. OCEAN — DAY

Wild killer whales are foraging for food.

> NARRATOR (V.O.)
> . . . One might assume that
> a salmon-eating killer whale
> would not be a lineage that
> should concern a diver.

ANGLE — Another pod of Southern Resident
killer whales.

DR. LANCE BARRETT-LENNARD (V.O.)
Southern Resident killer
whales are a fairly feisty
group . . .

BACK TO LANCE

DR. LANCE BARRETT-LENNARD
. . . They certainly have been
known on a number of occasions
to interact with other marine
mammal species to play with
them, effectively, to toy with
them . . .

PHOTO — Miracle swims away from a handler.

DR. LANCE BARRETT-LENNARD (V.O.)
. . . and it sometimes results
in the other critters dying.

PHOTO — Miracle surfaces at the Oak Bay pool.

NARRATOR (V.O.)
. . . So, because Miracle
was getting rough with
divers . . .

BACK AT MIRACLE'S POOL — A handler pours a
bucket of herring into her mouth after a
performance.

> NARRATOR (V.O.)
> . . . her handlers resorted to
> the use of a white stick. But
> the stick method may have also
> been a factor in Miracle's
> escalating aggressive
> behaviour.

PHOTO — Miracle, head out of the water, is being trained.

> DR. LANCE BARRETT-LENNARD (V.O.)
> I don't think there is an
> aquarium in the world now
> that uses any kind of negative
> conditioning . . .

BACK TO LANCE

> DR. LANCE BARRETT-LENNARD
> . . . Killer whales are
> different, they are a lot like
> humans . . .

TIGHT ON MIRACLE — She turns quickly in the pool.

> DR. LANCE BARRETT-LENNARD (V.O.)
> . . . If you try and
> intimidate me . . .

Miracle lurks just under the surface.

                    DR. LANCE BARRETT-LENNARD (V.O.)
                    . . . then I can be submissive
                    or I can try and intimidate
                    you. They respond by trying to
                    intimidate you . . .

BACK TO LANCE

                    DR. LANCE BARRETT-LENNARD (V.O.)
                    . . . You can't win a fight
                    with them . . .

Miracle swims straight toward the edge.

                    DR. LANCE BARRETT-LENNARD (V.O.)
                    . . . You can't convince
                    them not to do something by
                    threatening them, it just
                    becomes a battle of the egos.

Larry pets Miracle as she goes by after
taking a herring from his hand.

BACK TO LARRY

                    LARRY MCINERNEY
                    At that time, I wasn't
                    going in the pool with her,
                    because . . .

PHOTO — Miracle's head out of the water,
mouth open, lots of teeth.

          LARRY MCINERNEY (V.O.)
   . . . she was getting
   dangerous . . .

Miracle twists underwater right below the
trainer platform.

          LARRY MCINERNEY (V.O.)
   . . . and I was worried
   that, that if I dropped that
   stick . . .

BACK TO PHOTO — The handler with the white
stick.

          LARRY MCINERNEY (V.O.)
   . . . I could be in real
   trouble, and I basically was
   inspecting the pools from
   outside.

PHOTO — Miracle shows her teeth.

                      FADE TO:

EXT. SEALAND POOL — EVENING

The vacant and closed facility is quiet. A
young Alexandra drops a herring to Miracle.

          ALEXANDRA MORTON (V.O.)
   I was watching Miracle. She
   had a fur seal that lived with
   her . . .

Miracle's pool friend, Shadow the fur seal, waits eagerly for food from a Sealand handler. (Photo credit: Rochelle Termehr)

PHOTO — A Sealand staffer feeds the fur seal, Shadow.

> ALEXANDRA MORTON (V.O.)
> . . . called Shadow, and ah, Shadow didn't come up . . .

PHOTO — Miracle underwater, panning up to see Shadow swimming above her.

> ALEXANDRA MORTON (V.O.)
> . . . didn't come up, and didn't come up. Suddenly I could hear him breathing underneath the dock where I was standing . . .

EXT. MIRACLE'S PEN (UNDERWATER) — DAY

An inner net is visible through an outer cargo net.

> ALEXANDRA MORTON (V.O.)
> . . . but I couldn't see him. And the net, he was outside the net, he was under the float now . . .

BACK TO ALEXANDRA

> ALEXANDRA MORTON
> . . . so I ran and got the staff, and they said, "Oh yeah, it happens all the time. Miracle pulls apart the net . . .

PHOTO — Miracle near the wall.

> ALEXANDRA MORTON (V.O.)
> . . . and the seal goes
> through the hole and gets
> caught between the two
> nets." . . .

BACK TO PHOTO — Miracle deep in the pool.

> ALEXANDRA MORTON (V.O.)
> . . . They said Miracle does
> this all the time. She knows
> that if she wrecks the net,
> a diver would come into the
> water and she likes the
> divers . . .

EXT. OAK BAY BEACH HOTEL POOL — DAY

A diver plays with her in the pool when she
was a baby.

THREE PHOTOS — First, Miracle and Shadow
together in the pool. And then, the handler
feeding shadow a fish. And finally, Shadow
looking for another fish.

> ALEXANDRA MORTON (V.O.)
> . . . A few weeks later, I
> went back for my regular
> observation periods and the
> fur seal was gone, and I said,
> "What happened to Shadow?" And
> they said, "Well, he drowned
> between the two nets." . . .

BACK TO ALEXANDRA

>   ALEXANDRA MORTON
>   . . . Which is exactly what
>   happened to Miracle.

                                   DISSOLVE TO:

INT. OCEAN — DAY

A net spans across the frame with the sun
penetrating through it.

ANGLE — The mesh, now closer, moves through
the water.

>   ANGUS MATTHEWS (V.O.)
>   There were those who wanted
>   the whale free . . .

BACK TO ANGUS

>   ANGUS MATTHEWS
>   On the other side . . .

BACK TO MIRACLE'S POOL — It's empty and
quiet.

>   ANGUS MATTHEWS (V.O)
>   . . . there were real concerns
>   about the design of the
>   pool . . .

ON A CREW — They are waiting for Miracle to
arrive by helicopter.

> ANGUS MATTHEWS (V.O.)
> . . . As one who is perhaps
> ultimately responsible for the
> condition of the pool . . .

A diver is in the pool with her just after
she arrived.

> ANGUS MATTHEWS (V.O.)
> . . . and we did inspections
> and cared for the pool and so
> on . . .

BACK TO CREW — They are watching Miracle just
after her arrival at the pool.

BACK TO ANGUS

> ANGUS MATTHEWS
> . . . I must say I did cling
> to the hope that it hadn't
> really been our fault, but
> maybe it was.

AT THE SEALAND POOL — A killer whale moves
slowly in one of the pools.

> LARRY MCINHERNEY (V.O.)
> It's never the one thing that
> gets you, it's a combination
> of things that get you. And it
> just so happens, they all came
> together at a point . . .

BACK TO LARRY

                    LARRY MCINERNEY
           . . . where an accident
           happened . . .

PHOTO — Miracle underwater, plump and sassy.

                 LARRY MCINERNEY (V.O.)
           . . . At the time, Miracle was
           doing damage to her net . . .

ANGLE — From the cargo net, slowly moving
toward the chain-link fence.

                 LARRY MCINERNEY (V.O.)
           . . . Basically there was
           two nets. There was an outer
           orange cargo net and there was
           a chain-link fence . . .

FROM UNDER THE WHARF — The two nets are
spaced apart.

                 LARRY MCINERNEY (V.O.)
           . . . What she used to do, she
           used to get a hold of the
           cargo net which was quite
           close to the chain-link . . .

PHOTO — Miracle is at the bottom.

                 LARRY MCINERNEY (V.O.)
           . . . fence at both ends of
           the pool . . .

ANGLE — There is a huge hole in the chain-link fence.

> LARRY MCINERNEY (V.O.)
> . . . She'd pull on it and mushroom a hole that was maybe, oh, a couple of feet across . . .

PHOTO — Miracle underwater, looking up toward the surface.

> LARRY MCINERNEY (V.O.)
> . . . So they decided that we'd reinforce it with . . .

ON SOME THICK LINKS

> LARRY MCINERENY (V.O.)
> . . . heavy-gauge chain-link fence at the points where she was doing the damage, which was basically at both ends of the pool . . .

BACK TO HOLE — It looks eerie and is covered with shadows.

> LARRY MCINERNEY (V.O.)
> . . . I remember going and having a meeting with Bob and saying, "If she gets through that net, she's probably going to drown, because she's going to get entangled in that net."

EXT. OAK BAY BEACH HOTEL POOL (2000) — DAY

Angus Matthews slowly walks along the top of
the pool wall.

Suddenly Miracle is back swimming in the
pool.

Young Angus is on the edge of the pool and he
chuckles at little Miracle swimming in the
pool.

> ANGUS MATTHEWS (V.O.)
> I went underwater and for the
> first time and saw this sad,
> sad sight of . . .

BACK TO ANGUS

> ANGUS MATTHEWS
> . . . this whale in the net,
> halfway through the net. Um, I
> realized that it had all come
> to a tragic end.

TWO PHOTOS — Miracle leaps high into the
air at her new pool. Miracle underwater and
looking healthy.

BACK TO LARRY — He's feeding little Miracle
at the old pool.

> LARRY MCINERNEY (V.O.)
> We were getting threats . . .

BACK TO LARRY

                     LARRY MCINERNEY
        . . . from people who were
        going to cut the net, and I
        suspect . . .

TWO PHOTOS — First of Miracle in the old pool
and then of Miracle leaping in the new pool.

                   LARRY MCINERNEY (V.O.)
        . . . that's probably the
        reason why that net was left
        in place.

EXT. MIRACLE'S SEALAND POOL — DAY

Miracle plays with a big red ball.

                     NARRATOR (V.O.)
        In the end, Miracle's death
        was not the result of a
        bungled plot to free her. It
        was simply an accident . . .

PHOTO — Miracle spy hops.

                     NARRATOR (V.O.)
        . . . An accident brought
        about by a set of
        circumstances that included
        the design of the pool, the
        whale's behaviour . . .

UNDERWATER — Two divers swim toward a chain-
link fence.

> NARRATOR (V.O.)
> . . . the threat of
> environmental activism and
> human error . . .

Miracle leaps high into the air.

> NARRATOR (V.O.)
> . . . Miracle played a major
> part in shifting public
> sentiment regarding killer
> whales . . .

BACK TO MENZIES BAY — A weak Miracle
approaches, covered in algae.

> NARRATOR (V.O.)
> . . . from fear and hatred to
> admiration and awe . . .

BACK TO OAK BAY POOL — A diver plays with
Miracle, who takes a fish from a hand.

> NARRATOR (V.O.)
> And our understanding of the
> killer whale population off
> the Pacific coast has . . .

Miracle is on the foam pad with the Sealand
team attending to her.

                    NARRATOR (V.O.)
          . . . improved so much that
          experts were able to reunite
          the baby killer whale . . .

MONTAGE — Killer whales in the wild.

                    NARRATOR (V.O.)
          . . . Springer with her pod
          after a prolonged separation.
          But another juvenile who
          wanted to play with humans was
          not so lucky. Luna, who became
          caught between well-meaning,
          but conflicting groups of
          humans, died when he was . . .

BACK TO BILL'S BOAT — The propeller is
spinning up to speed.

                    NARRATOR (V.O.)
          . . . fatally struck by a boat
          propeller. So for situations
          like Miracle's . . .

A pod of killer whales rises up for a breath.

                    NARRATOR (V.O.)
          . . . have we made
          progress? . . .

INT. OCEAN — DAY

Killer whales disappear into the green murky
water.

> NARRATOR (V.O.)
> . . . How do we protect wild
> creatures from our politics
> and human frailties and still
> allow us to tap into one of
> the things that makes us human
> — compassion? . . .

CLOSE — They draw out some blood from
Miracle's tail.

> NARRATOR (V.O.)
> And will we ever be able to
> know, with certainty, when
> it's right to keep an animal
> safe and . . .

ANGLE — Bill is at the old pool, waist-deep
in water and feeding Miracle.

> NARRATOR (V.O.)
> . . . when it's right to help
> it and then set it free?

EXT. OAK BAY BEACH HOTEL POOL — DAY

Miracle takes a fish from Bill's fingers.

> BILL DAVIS (V.O.)
> She still remembered me . . .

BACK TO BILL

Bill Davis reaches out and touches Miracle's fin during one of her practice performances at Sealand. (Photo credit: Rochelle Termehr)

                    BILL DAVIS
          . . . but as time went on, she
          had so many people that were
          closer to her by that time. I
          believe they got more attached
          to her than she was to me by
          that time . . .

BACK TO THE OLD POOL

Bill leans over to feed Miracle and scratch
her belly.

                    BILL DAVIS (V.O.)
          . . . But I don't think
          she ever forgot me by any
          means . . .

Bill feeds her another herring.

                    BILL DAVIS (V.O.)
          . . . She always remembered me
          from back when she was really
          in trouble.

EXT. SEALAND POOL — DAY

Bill Davis leans over the pool. Miracle comes
up to him for a scratch. He pets her while
she lies beside him in the pool. Then, she
finally comes up and kisses her old friend on
the cheek.

And we freeze on that moment.

TAIL CREDITS

And the music takes us through to . . .

THE END

Bill Davis gives Miracle a hug after visiting her at her new home at Sealand of the Pacific. The bond between Miracle and her rescuer remained strong throughout her life. She never forgot Bill. (Photo credit: Bill Davis)

Acknowledgements

I would like to extend my sincere thanks to all of the interviewees who gave generously of their time, namely, William (Bill) Davis, Angus Matthews, Paul Watson, Patrick Moore, Alexandra Morton, Dr. Allan Hoey, Robert (Bob) Wright, Dr. Lance Barret-Lennard, Graeme Ellis, Dr. Peter Ross, Dr. John Ford, Dr. Tim Andrews, Peter Termehr, Grant Thompson, and Cathy Denny. Their thoughts and knowledge about Miracle's story and Pacific Coast orcas was indispensable and allowed me to pursue a deeper understanding of the story.

A great big thanks to my crew, especially Goran Basaric (Director of Photography), Maja Zdanowski (Editor), and Heather Kemski (Composer), whose work and talents brought the story to life with authenticity, accuracy, and emotional impact. Also a big thanks to Rob Neilson for his post-production skills in remastering the original film.

I would also like to thank all of those who shared images and footage from their personal archives (Peter Termehr, Rochelle Termehr, William (Bill) Davis, Grant Thompson, Alexandra Morton, Robert Webber, Graeme Ellis, Dr. Tag Gornall, Tim Andrews, and Wilma Thompson). That was not only important to taking us all back to the story as it happened, but also gave me crucial insights into the order of the events. I would also like to thank Sandra Parrish (Campbell River Museum), Kelly-Ann Tarkington (Royal BC Museum), and Colin Preston (CBC Archive) for their support and assistance in navigating their respective archives. Archives are crucial to documentary film makers, and without the dedicated staff that manage these resources, documentaries would just not be possible.

A great big thanks to Jan Westendorp for her amazing skill and guidance in managing the design and publishing of this book. And to Lesley

Cameron, whose terrific and prompt story editing kept the book project moving forward and made this a dream project to work on.

Finally, to my family who puts up with all those blank stares and the many days I spend squirrelled away in my office. I find the creative process so rewarding, but it can be all-encompassing and disruptive to normal life. Thanks for your patience and support.

www.ingramcontent.com/pod-product-compliance
Lightning Source LLC
Chambersburg PA
CBHW060323030426
42336CB00011B/1176